Stand Out Basic

Standards-Based English

Rob Jenkins

Staci Sabbagh Johnson

THOMSON

™

HEINLE

Australia • Canada • Mexico • Singapore • Spain • United Kingdom • United States

Stand Out Basic
Standards-Based English

Rob Jenkins and Staci Sabbagh Johnson

Publisher, Adult and Academic ESL
James W. Brown

Senior Acquisitions Editor
Sherrise Roehr

Director of Product Development
Anita Raducanu

Developmental Editor
Sarah Barnicle

Editorial Assistants
Katherine Reilly, John Hicks

Marketing Manager
Donna Lee Kennedy

Director, Global ESL Training & Development
Evelyn Nelson

Senior Production Editor
Maryellen Killeen

Senior Manufacturing Coordinator
Mary Beth Hennebury

Photo Researcher
Sheri Blaney

Senior Developmental Editor
Ingrid Wisniewska

Project Manager
Tünde A. Dewey

Compositor
Pre-Press Company, Inc.

Text Printer/Binder
RR Donnelley

Cover Printer
Phoenix Color Corporation

Designers
Elise Kaiser
Julia Gecha

Cover Designer
Gina Petti

Illustrators
James Edwards represented by Sheryl Beranbaum
Leo Cultura of Racketshop Design Studio, Philippines
Ray Medici
Vilma Ortiz-Dillon
Scott MacNeill

Cover Art
Diana Ong/SuperStock

For more information, contact Thomson Heinle 25 Thomson Place, Boston, MA 02210; or you can visit our Internet site at
http://www.heinle.com

For permission to use material from this text or product, contact us by:
Tel   1-800-730-2214
Fax   1-800-730-2215
www.thomsonrights.com

Library of Congress Catalog-in-Publication Data

Jenkins, Rob.
  Stand out Basic : standards-based English / by Rob Jenkins and Staci Sabbagh Johnson.—1st ed. p. cm.
  Includes index.
  ISBN 1-41300-164-5
    1. English language—Textbooks for foreign speakers. I. Title: Stand out basic. II. Johnson, Staci Sabbagh. III. Title.

PE1128 .J435 2002
428.2'4—dc21
                                    2001039891

CREDITS

PHOTO CREDITS

Frontmatter
P. v: © Courtney Sabbagh

Pre-Unit
P. P3: © David Young-Wolff/Photo Edit
P. P5, T: © Mark Segal/Index Stock Imagery
P. P5, B: © Hemera Photo Objects

Unit 1
P. 8, T: © Mitch Diamond/Index Stock Imagery
P. 8, M: © ImageSource/SuperStock
P. 8, B: © Bananastock/Alamy
P. 10: © Bill Aron/PhotoEdit
P. 11, 2nd from top: © Bob Mahoney/The Image Works
P. 11, B: © Heinle, Thomson Learning
P. 14: © ThinkStock LL/Index Stock Imagery
P. 18, TL: © David Urbina/Index Stock Imagery
P. 18, TR: © David Katzenstein/CORBIS
P. 18, BL: © Joe Carini/Index Stock Imagery

Unit 2
P. 24, TL: © Bob Krist/CORBIS
P. 24, ML: © Tom Wagner/CORBIS SABA
P. 24, BL: © Walter Bibikow/Jon Arnold Images/Alamy
P. 24, TR: © George Goodwin/SuperStock
P. 24, MR: © Bilderberg/Aurora
P. 24, BR: © David Turnley/CORBIS
P. 28, Top objects: © Hemera Photo Objects
P. 28, BL: © James Darell/Photodisc/Getty Images
P. 28, BM: © Ken Reld/Image Bank/Getty Images
P. 28, BR: © Gary Conner/PhotoEdit
P. 32: © Hemera Photo Objects
P. 36, TL: © Dan Bigelow/Image Bank/Getty Images
P. 36, BL: © Hemera Photo Objects
P. 36, TR: © Amy Etra/PhotoEdit
P. 36, BR: © Karen Preuss/The Image Works
P. 38, T: © Cleve Bryant/Photoedit
P. 38, TM: © Gareth Brown/CORBIS
P. 38, BM: © Ron Chapple/ThinkStock/Alamy
P. 38, B: © Michael Newman/PhotoEdit

Unit 3
P. 48, all: © Hemera Photo Objects except 4th from top: © Burke/Triolo Productions/Foodpix
P. 53, all: © Hemera Photo Objects

Unit 4
P. 62, Clockwise: shoes: © Hemera Photo Objects; shirt: © David Young-Wolff/PhotoEdit; pants, socks: © Hemera Photo Objects; dress and blouse: © John Coletti; shorts and sweater: © Hemera Photo Objects; coat: © John Coletti
P. 67, 68, money bills: ©John Coletti; coins: ©Getty Images.
P. 72, TL, BL: © John Coletti
P. 72, TR: © Hemera Photo Objects

Unit 5
P. 86, TL: © Kevin Peterson/Photodisc/Getty Images
P. 86, TM, TR: © Heinle, Thomson Learning
P. 88, TL: © Jonathan Nourok/PhotoEdit
P. 88 ML: © Bonnie Kamin/PhotoEdit
P. 88, BL: © Dennis MacDonald/PhotoEdit
P. 88, TR: © Amy Etra/PhotoEdit
P. 88, BR: © Hemera Photo Objects
P. 90, TL: © Image Source/Alamy
P. 90, TM: © Michael Newman/PhotoEdit
P. 90, TR: © Ryan McVay/ Photodisc/ Getty Images
P. 97, TL: © Gary Connor/PhotoEdit
P. 97, TR: © Photodisc/Getty Images

Unit 6
P. 104, TL: © BananaStock Ltd.
P. 104, TM: © BananaStock Ltd.
P. 104, TR: © Ian O'Leary/Stone/Getty Images
P. 104, BL: © BananaStock Ltd.
P. 104, BR: © Alan Thornton/Stone/Getty Images
P. 114, © John Henley/CORBIS
P. 115, TL: © Mark Anderson/Rubberball/Alamy
P. 115, TM,: © Mary Kate Demy/PhotoEdit
P. 115, TR: © Jim Cummins/CORBIS

Unit 7
P. 124 TL: © Jim Pickerell/Stock Connection, Inc./Alamy
P: 124 TR: © Mark Andersen/RubberBall/Alamy
P. 124 BL: © Christina Micek
P. 124 BR: © Digital Vision/Getty Images
P. 127 BL: © Bob Daemmrich/The Image Works
P. 127, BR: © Charles Gupton/CORBIS
P. 128, TL: © David Young-Wolff/PhotoEdit
P. 128, TR: © Spencer Grant /PhotoEdit
P. 134: © PhotoDisc/Getty Images
P. 137, B: © Michael Newman/PhotoEdit

Unit 8
P. 147: © Christina Micek
P. 150: © View Stock China/Alamy
P. 153: © Charles Gupton/CORBIS

ACKNOWLEDGMENTS

The authors and publisher would like to thank the following reviewers, consultants, and participants in focus groups:

Elizabeth Aderman
New York City Board of Education, New York, NY

Sharon Baker
Roseville Adult School, Roseville, CA

Lillian Barredo
Stockton School for Adults, Stockton, CA

Linda Boice
Elk Grove Adult Education, Elk Grove, CA

Chan Bostwick
Los Angeles Unified School District, Los Angeles, CA

Rose Cantu
John Jay High School, San Antonio, TX

Toni Chapralis
Fremont School for Adults, Sacramento, CA

Melanie Chitwood
Miami-Dade Community College, Miami, FL

Geri Creamer
Stockton School for Adults, Stockton, CA

Stephanie Daubar
Harry W. Brewster Technical Center, Tampa, FL

Irene Dennis
San Antonio College, San Antonio, TX

Eileen Duffell
P.S. 64, New York, NY

Nancy Dunlap
Northside Independent School District, San Antonio, TX

Gloria Eriksson
Old Marshall Adult Education Center, Sacramento, CA

Marti Estrin
Santa Rosa Junior College, Santa Rosa, CA

Lawrence Fish
Shorefront YM-YWHA English Language Program, Brooklyn, NY

Victoria Florit
Miami-Dade Community College, Miami, FL

Rhoda Gilbert
New York City Board of Education, New York, NY

Kathleen Jimenez
Miami-Dade Community College, Miami, FL

Nancy Jordan
John Jay High School Adult Education, San Antonio, TX

Renee Klosz
Lindsey Hopkins Technical Education Center, Miami, FL

David Lauter
Stockton School for Adults, Stockton, CA

Patricia Long
Old Marshall Adult Education Center, Sacramento, CA

Daniel Loos
Seattle Community College, Seattle, WA

Maria Miranda
Lindsey Hopkins Technical Education Center, Miami, FL

Karen Moore
Stockton School for Adults, Stockton, CA

George Myskiw
Malcolm X College, Chicago, IL

Marta Pitt
Lindsey Hopkins Technical Education Center, Miami, FL

Sylvia Rambach
Stockton School for Adults, Stockton, CA

Charleen Richardson
San Antonio College, San Antonio, TX

Eric Rosenbaum
Bronx Community College, New York, NY

Laura Rowley
Old Marshall Adult Education Center, Sacramento, CA

Amy Schneider
Pacoima Skills Center, Pacoima, CA

Sr. M. B. Theresa Spittle
Stockton School for Adults, Stockton, CA

Andre Sutton
Belmont Adult School, Los Angeles, CA

Jennifer Swoyer
Northside Independent School District, San Antonio, TX

Claire Valier
Palm Beach County School District, West Palm Beach, FL

The authors would like to thank Joel and Rosanne for believing in us, Eric for seeing our vision, Nancy and Sherrise for going to bat for us, and Jim, Ingrid, and Sarah for making the book a reality.

Rob Jenkins

Staci Sabbagh Johnson

I love teaching. I love to see the expressions on my students' faces when the light goes on and their eyes show such sincere joy of learning. I knew the first time I stepped into an ESL classroom that this was where I needed to be and I have never questioned that resolution. I have worked in business, sales, and publishing, and I've found challenge in all, but nothing can compare to the satisfaction of reaching people in such a personal way.

Thanks to my family who have put up with late hours and early mornings, my friends at church who support me, and everyone at Santa Ana College, School of Continuing Education who believe in me and are a source of tremendous inspiration.

Ever since I can remember, I've been fascinated with other cultures and languages. I love to travel and every place I go, the first thing I want to do is meet the people, learn their language, and understand their culture. Becoming an ESL teacher was a perfect way to turn what I love to do into my profession. There's nothing more incredible than the exchange of teaching and learning from one another that goes on in an ESL classroom. And there's nothing more rewarding than helping a student succeed.

I would especially like to thank Mom, Dad, CJ, Tete, Eric, my close friends, and my Santa Ana College, School of Continuing Education family. Your love and support inspired me to do something I never imagined I could. And Rob, thank you for trusting me to be part of such an amazing project.

We are lesson plan enthusiasts! We have learned that good lesson planning makes for effective teaching and, more importantly, good learning. We also believe that learning is stimulated by task-oriented activities in which students find themselves critically laboring over decisions and negotiating meaning from their own personal perspectives.

The need to write **Stand Out** came to us as we were leading a series of teacher workshops on project-based simulations designed to help students apply what they have learned. We began to teach lesson planning within our workshops in order to help teachers see how they could incorporate the activities more effectively. Even though teachers showed great interest in both the projects and planning, they often complained that lesson planning took too much time that they simply didn't have. Another obstacle was that the books available to the instructors were not conducive to planning lessons.

We decided to write our own materials by first writing lesson plans that met specific student-performance objectives. Then we developed the student pages that were needed to make the lesson plans work in the classroom. The student book only came together after the plans! Writing over 300 lesson plans has been a tremendous challenge and has helped us evaluate our own teaching and approach. It is our hope that others will discover the benefits of always following a plan in the classroom and incorporating the strategies we have included in these materials.

ABOUT THE SERIES

The **Stand Out** series is designed to facilitate *active* learning while challenging students to build a nurturing and effective learning community.

The student books are divided into eight distinct units, mirroring competency areas most useful to newcomers. These areas are outlined in CASAS assessment programs and different state model standards for adults. Each unit in *Stand Out Basic* is then divided into five lessons, a review, and a team project activity. Lessons are driven by performance objectives and are filled with challenging activities that progress from teacher-presented to student-centered tasks.

SUPPLEMENTAL MATERIALS

- The *Stand Out Basic Lesson Planner* is in full color with 60 complete lesson plans, taking the instructor through each stage of a lesson from warm-up and review through application.

- The *Stand Out Basic Activity Bank CD-ROM* has an abundance of customizable worksheets. Print or download and modify what you need for your particular class, or use the printed book as a workbook for in-class use and homework.

- The *Stand Out Basic Grammar Challenge* is a workbook that gives additional grammar explanation and practice in context.

- The *Stand Out* ExamView ® Pro *Test Bank CD-ROM* allows you to customize pre- and post-tests for each unit as well as a pre- and post-test for the book.

- Listening scripts are found in the back of the student book and the Lesson Planner. Cassette tapes and CDs are available with focused listening activities described in the Lesson Planner.

STAND OUT BASIC LESSON PLANNER

The *Stand Out Basic Lesson Planner* is a new and innovative approach. As many seasoned teachers know, good lesson planning can make a substantial difference in the classroom. Students continue coming to class, understanding, applying, and remembering more of what they learn. They are more confident in their learning when good lesson planning techniques are incorporated.

We have developed lesson plans that are designed to be used each day and to reduce preparation time. The planner includes:

- Standard lesson progression (Warm-up and Review, Introduction, Presentation, Practice, Evaluation, and Application)
- A creative and complete way to approach varied class lengths so that each lesson will work within a class period.
- 180 hours of classroom activities
- Time suggestions for each activity
- Pedagogical comments
- Space for teacher notes and future planning
- Identification of SCANS, EFF, and CASAS standards

USER QUESTIONS ABOUT *STAND OUT*

- **What are SCANS and EFF and how do they integrate into the book?**
  SCANS is the Secretary's Commission on Achieving Necessary Skills. SCANS was developed to encourage students to prepare for the workplace. The standards developed through SCANS have been incorporated throughout the **Stand Out** student books and components.

  Stand Out addresses SCANS a little differently than do other books. SCANS standards elicit effective teaching strategies by incorporating essential skills such as critical thinking and group work. We have incorporated SCANS standards in every lesson, not isolating these standards in the work unit, as is typically done.

  EFF, or Equipped for the Future, is a set of standards established to address students' roles as parents, workers, and citizens, with a vision of student literacy and lifelong learning. **Stand Out** addresses these standards and integrates them into the materials in a way similar to SCANS.

- **What about CASAS?** The federal government has mandated that states show student outcomes as a prerequisite to receiving funding. Some states have incorporated the **C**omprehensive **A**dult **S**tudent **A**ssessment **S**ystem (CASAS) testing to standardize agency reporting. Unfortunately, since many of our students are unfamiliar with standardized testing and therefore struggle with it, adult schools need to develop lesson plans to address specific concerns. **Stand Out** was developed with careful attention to CASAS skill areas in most lessons and performance objectives.

- **Are the tasks too challenging for my students?**
  Students learn by doing and learn more when challenged. **Stand Out** provides tasks that encourage critical thinking in a variety of ways. The tasks in each lesson move from teacher-directed to student-centered so the learner clearly understands what's expected and is willing to "take a risk." The lessons are expected to be challenging. In this way, students learn that when they work together as a learning community, anything becomes possible. The satisfaction of accomplishing something both as an individual and as a member of a team results in greater confidence and effective learning.

- **Do I need to understand lesson planning to teach from the student book?** If you don't understand lesson planning when you start, you will when you finish! Teaching from **Stand Out** is like a course on lesson planning, especially if you use the Lesson Planner on a daily basis.

  Stand Out does *stand out* because, when we developed this series, we first established performance objectives for each lesson. Then we designed lesson plans, followed by student book pages. The introduction to each lesson varies because different objectives demand different approaches. **Stand Out's** variety of tasks makes learning more interesting for the student.

- **What are team projects?** The final lesson of each unit is a **team project**. This is often a team simulation that incorporates the objectives of the unit and provides an additional opportunity for students to actively apply what they have learned. The project allows students to produce something that represents their progress in learning. These end-of-unit projects were created with a variety of learning styles and individual skills in mind. The team projects can be skipped or simplified, but we encourage instructors to implement them, enriching the overall student experience.

- **What do you mean by a customizable Activity Bank?** Every class, student, teacher, and approach is different. Since no one textbook can meet all these differences, the *Stand Out Activity Bank CD-ROM* allows you to customize **Stand Out** for your class. You can copy different activities and worksheets from the CD-ROM to your hard drive and then:
  - change items in supplemental vocabulary, grammar, and life skill activities;

- personalize activities with student names and popular locations in your area;

- extend every lesson with additional practice where you feel it is most needed.

- **Is *Stand Out* grammar-based or competency-based?**
  Stand Out is a competency-based series; however, students are exposed to basic grammar structures. We believe that grammar instruction in context is extremely important. Grammar structures are periodically identified as principal lesson objectives. Students are first provided with context that incorporates the grammar, followed by an explanation and practice. At this level, we expect students to learn basic structures but we do not expect them to acquire them. It has been our experience that students are exposed several times within their learning experience to language structures before they actually acquire them. For teachers who want to enhance grammar instruction, the *Activity Bank CD-ROM* and/or the *Grammar Challenge* workbooks provide ample opportunities.

  The six competencies that drive **Stand Out** are basic communication, consumer economics, community resources, health, occupational knowledge, and lifelong learning (government and law replace lifelong learning in Books 3 and 4).

- **Are there enough activities so I don't have to supplement?**
  Stand Out stands alone in providing 160 hours of instruction and activities, even without the additional suggestions in the Lesson Planner. The Lesson Planner also shows you how to streamline lessons to provide 90 hours of classwork and still have thorough lessons if you meet less often. When supplementing with the *Stand Out Activity Bank CD-ROM*, the ExamView® Pro *Test Bank CD-ROM*, and the *Stand Out Grammar Challenge* workbook, you gain unlimited opportunities to extend class hours and provide activities related directly to each lesson objective. Calculate how many hours your class meets in a semester and look to **Stand Out** to address the full class experience.

  Stand Out is a comprehensive approach to adult language learning, meeting needs of students and instructors completely and effectively.

CONTENTS

Theme	Unit and page number	Life Skills	Language Functions	Grammar	Vocabulary
	Pre-unit Welcome to Our Class *Page P2*	• Say alphabet and numbers • Write names and phone numbers • Follow classroom instructions	• Greet people • Say and understand letters • Say and understand numbers • Follow simple instructions	◆ *be* verb ◆ *Commands*	• Alphabet and numbers • *hello, hi, goodbye, bye* • Classroom vocabulary: *circle, bubble in, listen, point, practice, read, repeat, write*
Basic Communication	**1 Personal Information** *Page 1*	• Write names • Say and write numbers • Say and write the date • Read a calendar • Ask for marital status • Say and write addresses • Complete a school application • Complete forms	• Ask for and give personal information • Ask and answer questions about the date	• Subject pronouns • *be* verb • Contractions with *be* • *Wh-* questions with *be* • Possessive adjectives	• Months of the year, *month, day, year, week* • Marital status: *single, married, divorced* • Address vocabulary: *city, state, zip code, street, avenue, road*
	2 Our Class *Page 21*	• Ask where people are from • Describe the weather • Identify classroom activities • Tell time • Describe the classroom	• Ask for and give personal information • Describe actions • Tell time • Describe locations of objects • Talk about schedules	◆ *It is, It's* • Prepositions of location: *in, on, between, next to, in front of, in back of* ◆ Present continuous ◆ *Wh-* questions with *be*	• Weather vocabulary: *foggy, cloudy, rainy, windy, sunny, snowy, hot, cold* • Verbs: *listen, read, write, talk, sit, stand* • Classroom vocabulary: *desk, table, computer, book, file cabinet, trash can, bookcase*
Consumer Economics	**3 Food** *Page 41*	• Describe food and meals • Express hunger • Read ingredients on a recipe • Create a shopping list • Express wants and preferences • Plan meals	• Describe locations • Express needs • Express quantity • Express wants and preferences • Compare preferences	❖ Prepositions of location ❖ Contractions with *be* • Singular and plural nouns • Simple present with *like* • Negative form of *be*	• Food items • Meals: *breakfast, lunch, dinner* • Recipe vocabulary • Supermarket vocabulary: *dairy, fruit, vegetables, meat, fish* • Packaging vocabulary: *package, pound, jar*
	4 Clothing *Page 61*	• Describe what people wear • Describe clothing by color • Understand numbers and prices • Identify money • Count money • Read clothing receipts • Read newspaper advertisements • Write checks	• Make purchases in a store • Describe clothing • Count money • Ask about prices • Read receipts • Make a payment	• Singular and plural nouns • *There is/there are* • Articles (*a*) • Adjective/noun order ◆ Questions with *how much, how many*	• Clothing: *coat, dress, shirt, socks, blouse, shorts, shoes, sweater* • Colors: *red, yellow, blue, green, white, black* • Money: *dime, nickel, penny, quarter, dollar bill*

• Grammar points that are explicitly taught   ◆ Grammar points that are presented in context   ❖ Grammar points that are being recycled

EFF	SCANS (Workplace)	Math	CASAS
• Speak so others can understand • Listen actively	• Acquiring and evaluating information • Listening • Speaking • Writing • Sociability	• Write numerals 0–10 • Write telephone numbers	**1:** 0.1.1, 0.1.4 **2:** 0.1.1, 0.1.4 **3:** 0.1.1, 0.1.4, 0.2.1 **4:** 0.1.5
• Speak so others can understand • Listen actively • Cooperate with others	Many SCAN skills are incorporated in this unit with an emphasis on: • Acquiring and evaluating information • Basic Skills • Sociability • Seeing things in the mind's eye	• Write numerals 1–31 • Read and write dates in numerals	**1:** 0.1.1, 0.2.1 **2:** 0.1.2, 0.2.1, 2.3.2 **3:** 0.1.2, 0.2.1 **4:** 0.1.2, 0.2.1 **5:** 0.1.2, 0.2.1, 0.2.2 **R:** 0.1.1, 0.2.1 **TP:** 4.8.1, 4.8.5, 4.8.6
• Read with understanding • Convey ideas in writing • Speak so others can understand • Listen actively • Cooperate with others • Observe critically • Take responsibility for learning • Reflect and evaluate	Many SCAN skills are incorporated in this unit with an emphasis on: • Acquiring and evaluating information • Organizing and maintaining information • Interpreting and communicating information • Basic Skills	• Interpret a bar graph • Interpret measurements in inches • Tell time	**1:** 0.1.2, 0.2.1, 1.1.3, 4.6.5, 4.7.4, 4.8.7 **2:** 0.1.2, 0.2.1, 1.1.3, 2.3.3, 4.8.1, 7.4.8 **3:** 0.1.5 **4:** 0.2.1, 0.2.4, 2.3.1 **5:** 0.1.5 **R:** 0.1.2, 0.1.5, 0.2.1, 0.2.4, 2.3.1, 2.3.3 **TP:** 4.8.1, 4.8.5, 4.8.6
• Read with understanding • Convey ideas in writing • Speak so others can understand • Listen actively • Cooperate with others • Take responsibility for learning • Reflect and evaluate	Many SCAN skills are incorporated in this unit with an emphasis on: • Acquiring and evaluating information • Organizing and maintaining information • Interpreting and communicating information • Allocating human resources • Basic Skills • Seeing things in the mind's eye	• Use U.S. measurements: pounds • Express quantity: *a package of, a jar of* • Create Venn diagrams	**1:** 1.3.8 **2:** 1.3.8 **3:** 1.1.1, 1.3.8 **4:** 1.3.8, 3.5.2 **5:** 1.3.8, 3.5.2 **R:** 1.3.8 **TP:** 4.8.1, 4.8.5, 4.8.6
• Read with understanding • Convey ideas in writing • Speak so others can understand • Listen actively • Cooperate with others • Observe critically • Use math • Take responsibility for learning • Reflect and evaluate • Observe critically • Guide others	Many SCAN skills are incorporated in this unit with an emphasis on: • Acquiring and evaluating information • Organizing and maintaining information • Interpreting and communicating information • Basic Skills • Allocating money • Serving clients and customers	• Use U.S. measurements: clothing sizes • Maintain inventories • Count U.S. money • Understand numbers to 100 • Calculate totals • Write checks	**1:** 1.2.1, 1.3.9 **2:** 1.1.9, 1.2.1, 1.3.9 **3:** 1.1.6, 1.3.1, 1.3.9, 4.8.1, 6.1.1 **4:** 1.1.9, 1.2.1, 1.3.9, 4.8.3 **5:** 1.3.1, 1.3.9, 1.8.2 **R:** 1.1.9, 1.2.1, 1.3.1, 1.3.9, 1.8.2 **TP:** 4.8.1, 4.8.5, 4.8.6

CASAS: Numbers in bold indicate lesson numbers; **R** indicates review lesson; **TP** indicates team project.

CONTENTS

• Grammar points that are explicitly taught   ◆ Grammar points that are presented in context   ❖ Grammar points that are being recycled

EFF	SCANS (Workplace)	Math	CASAS
• Read with understanding • Convey ideas in writing • Speak so others can understand • Listen actively • Cooperate with others • Observe critically • Take responsibility for learning • Reflect and evaluate • Solve problems and make decisions	Many SCAN skills are incorporated in this unit with an emphasis on: • Acquiring and evaluating information • Organizing and maintaining information • Interpreting and communicating information • Basic Skills • Creative thinking • Participating as a member of a team	• Calculate distance on a map • Compare costs • Interpret a bar graph • Create a bar graph	**1:** 7.2.3 **2:** 1.4.1, 1.4.2 **3:** 2.2.3, 2.2.5,1.1.3, 6.7.2 **4:** 0.1.2, 0.2.4 **5:** 1.1.3, 1.9.1, 1.9.4, 2.2.1, 2.2.2, 2.5.4 **R:** 0.1.2, 1.1.3, 1.4.1, 1.9.4, 2.2.1, 2.2.2, 2.2.3, 2.5.4 **TP:** 4.8.1, 4.8.5, 4.8.6
• Read with understanding • Convey ideas in writing • Speak so others can understand • Listen actively • Cooperate with others • Observe critically • Take responsibility for learning • Reflect and evaluate • Advocate and influence	Most SCAN skills are incorporated in this unit with an emphasis on: • Acquiring and evaluating information • Organizing and maintaining information • Interpreting and communicating information • Basic Skills • Self-management • Responsibility	• Interpret schedules • Express frequency: *once a year, twice a week*	**1:** 3.1.1, 3.1.3 **2:** 0.1.2, 0.2.1, 3.1.1 **3:** 0.1.4 **4:** 2.3.1, 3.1.2, 3.3.1 **5:** 3.1.1 **R:** 3.1.1, 3.3.1, 3.4.2 **TP:** 4.8.1, 4.8.5, 4.8.6
• Read with understanding • Convey ideas in writing • Speak so others can understand • Listen actively • Cooperate with others • Advocate and influence • Resolve conflict and negotiate • Observe critically • Take responsibility for learning • Reflect and evaluate	Most SCAN skills are incorporated in this unit with an emphasis on: • Acquiring and evaluating information • Organizing and maintaining information • Interpreting and communicating information • Basic Skills • Self-management	• Interpret charts • Create a Venn diagram	**1:** 0.2.1, 4.1.8 **2:** 0.1.6, 4.8.1 **3:** 4.1.3, 4.1.8, 4.4.4 **4:** 0.2.3, 4.6.2 **5:** 4.4.4, 4.8.1, 4.8.3 **R:** 4.1.3, 4.1.8, 4.4.4 **TP:** 4.8.1, 4.8.5, 4.8.6
• Read with understanding • Convey ideas in writing • Speak so others can understand • Listen actively • Cooperate with others • Resolve conflict and negotiate • Observe critically • Take responsibility for learning • Reflect and evaluate	Most SCAN skills are incorporated in this unit with an emphasis on: • Acquiring and evaluating information • Organizing and maintaining information • Interpreting and communicating information • Basic Skills • Self-management	• Use U.S. measurements: *inches* • Create a bar graph • Create a schedule • Identify quantities and sizes • Calculate totals • Read telephone numbers • Read bar graphs	**1:** 0.2.1, 0.2.2, 7.1.4 **2:** 1.1.6, 1.2.1, 1.3.1, 1.6.4, 7.1.4 **3:** 2.1.1, 2.2.1, 7.1.4 **4:** 0.2.1, 3.5.9, 6.7.2, 7.1.1, 7.1.2, 7.1.4 **5:** 4.4.1, 4.4.4, 7.1.1, 7.1.4 **R:** 1.2.1, 2.2.1, 7.1.1, 7.1.3, 7.1.4 **TP:** 4.8.1, 4.8.5, 4.8.6

CASAS: Numbers in bold indicate lesson numbers; **R** indicates review lesson; **TP** indicates team project.

Guide to Stand Out Basic

Meeting the Standards has never been easier!

Stand Out is an easy-to-use, standards-based series for adult students that teaches the English skills necessary to be a successful worker, parent, and citizen.

- **Goals:** Provide a road map of learning for the student.

- **Contextualization:** Presents language in a natural context.

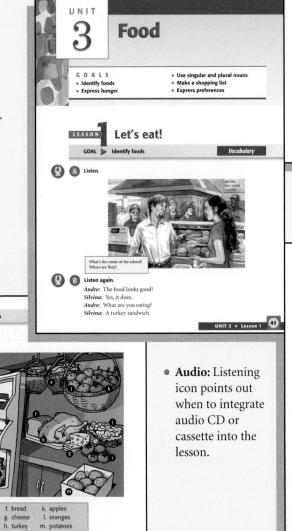

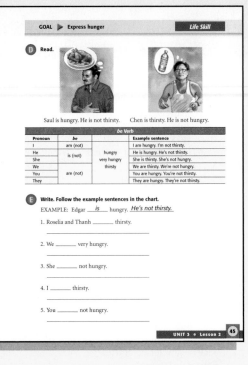

- **Audio:** Listening icon points out when to integrate audio CD or cassette into the lesson.

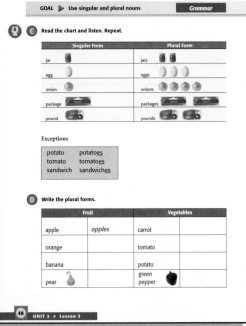

- **Grammar:** Clear explanations are followed by immediate use with reading and writing.

- **Vocabulary:** Introduces key words visually and aurally.

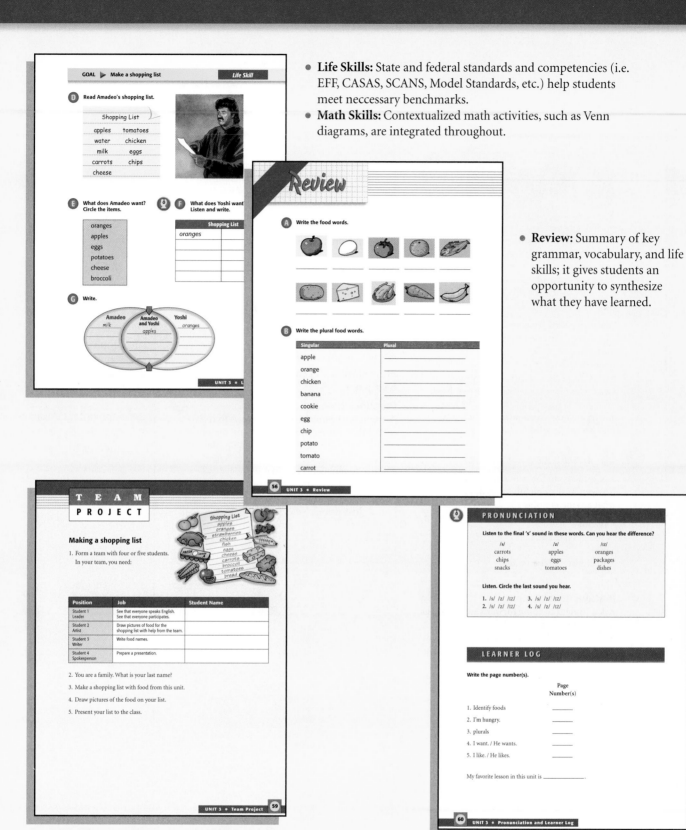

- **Life Skills:** State and federal standards and competencies (i.e. EFF, CASAS, SCANS, Model Standards, etc.) help students meet neccessary benchmarks.
- **Math Skills:** Contextualized math activities, such as Venn diagrams, are integrated throughout.

- **Review:** Summary of key grammar, vocabulary, and life skills; it gives students an opportunity to synthesize what they have learned.

- **Team Projects:** Project-based activities utilize SCANS competencies (e.g., making decisions, working on a team, developing interpersonal skills, etc.) and provide motivation for students.

- **Pronunciation:** Targets and corrects specific pronunciation problems.
- **Learning Log:** Final section of each unit provides opportunity for learner self-assessment.

LESSON PLAN

Objective:
Identify foods
Key vocabulary:
sandwich, mayonnaise, milk, water, eggs, chicken, bread, turkey, cheese, lettuce, tomatoes, apples, bananas, oranges, potatoes, breakfast, lunch, dinner

 Pre-Assessment: Use the *Stand Out Basic* ExamView® Pro *Test Bank* for Unit 3. *(optional)*

Warm-up and Review: 10–15 min.
Ask students to open their books and look at the picture of Andre and Silvina. Ask students where they think the two students are from for review of the last unit. Allow students to guess. There is no one correct answer. Next, ask students where they think Andre and Silvina are now. Ask students what foods they like. Make a list on the board.

  A   Listen. *(Audio CD, Track 50)*

Ask students to listen to a conversation between Andre and Silvina. Ask students what Silvina is eating.

| Agenda |
| (Today's day and date) _____ / _____ / _____ |
| Food |
| Breakfast, lunch, dinner |

Introduction: 10 min.
Ask a student to come forward and write the day of the week and the date on the board below the word Agenda. Continue with the vocabulary practice from the warm-up by asking

students if they like American food. Ask individuals where they are from and to name one food item from their country. A student from Mexico may say *enchiladas*, for example.

State the objective: *Today we will identify food.*

Presentation 1: 30–45 min.

B   Listen again. *(Audio CD, Track 50)*

Play the recording again and ask students to read the dialog between Silvina and Andre. Ask students what you need to make a turkey sandwich. At this level, they may not completely understand. Lead them through the different ingredients of a turkey sandwich.

Presentation 1 is continued on the next page.

Pronunciation:
An *optional* pronunciation activity is found on the final page of this unit. This pronunciation activity may be introduced during any lesson in this unit, especially if students need practice pronouncing the final sounds of "s." Go to page 60a for Pronunciation.

| Instructor's Notes for Lesson 1 |
| _____ |
| _____ |
| _____ |
| _____ |
| _____ |

- **Lesson Plan:** A complete lesson plan for each page in the student book using nationally accepted curriculum design

- **Pacing Guides:** Class-length icons offer three different pacing strategies.

- **CD Icon:** Points out when to use supplemental activities found on the *Activity Bank CD-ROM*

- Supplemental warm-up activities prepare students for lessons.

Plan Meals: Lunch

A. Read the menu.

Chicago Café
Lunch Menu

Main Course		Side Dish		Beverage	
Chicken sandwich	$4	Corn	$1	Water	$1
Roast beef sandwich	$5	Green beans	$1	Milk	$1
Cheese sandwich	$4	Baked potato	$2	Soda	$1
Spaghetti	$4	French fries	$1	Coffee	$1
		Rice	$1	Orange Juice	$1

B. Read and practice.

Waiter: Can I take your order?
Customer: Yes. I want a <u>chicken sandwich, French fries, and water</u>, please.
Waiter: OK, that's a <u>chicken sandwich, French fries, and water</u>, right?
Customer: Right.

C. Practice with two students and write the order.

Order	
Table <u>4</u>	
Server: *(Your name)* _____	
	Total

Order	
Table <u>6</u>	
Server: *(Your name)* _____	
	Total

Heinle, a division of Thomson Learning © 2005
Stand Out Basic Activity Bank

CHALLENGE 4 ▶ Simple present of *like* and *want*

Simple present		
Pronoun	**Verb**	**Example sentence**
I, you, we, they	like	I like chocolate.
	want	We want fruit salad.
he, she, it	likes	She likes ice cream.
	wants	He wants potato chips.

A Write *like* or *likes*.

1. Amadeo _____ cookies.
2. Chen _____ apple pie.
3. Saul _____ chocolate sundaes.

4. Amadeo, Chen, and Saul _____ desserts.

B Bubble in the correct answer.

		like	likes
EXAMPLE:	Maria _____ desserts.	○ like	● likes
1.	Maria _____ ice cream.	○ like	○ likes
2.	Saul _____ cookies.	○ like	○ likes
3.	I _____ candy.	○ like	○ likes
4.	They _____ apple pie.	○ like	○ likes
5.	You _____ fruit.	○ like	○ likes
6.	Andre and Silvina _____ sundaes.	○ like	○ likes
7.	He _____ cake.	○ like	○ likes
8.	We _____ chocolate.	○ like	○ likes
9.	My partner _____ chocolate ice cream.	○ like	○ likes
10.	My partner and I _____ chocolate cake.	○ like	○ likes

Unit 3 Post-Assessment

Multiple Choice

Choose.

____ 1. I _____ thirsty.
   a. are
   b. is
   c. am

____ 2. They _____ very hungry.
   a. are
   b. is
   c. am

____ 3. She _____ thirsty.
   a. isn't
   b. aren't
   c. am not

____ 4. We _____ hungry.
   a. am not
   b. isn't
   c. aren't

____ 5. You _____ cookies.
   a. like
   b. liking
   c. likes

Short Answer

Write am, is, or are.

6. I _____ hungry.

7. Andre _____ thirsty.

8. We _____ very thirsty.

Problem

Write.

9. What do you eat for lunch? _____

10. What do you eat for dinner? _____

▲ **Activity Bank CD-ROM:** Provides hours of motivating and creative reinforcement activities to supplement the student book lessons. Literacy activities are available to supplement initial units. Instructors can download activities and adapt them to student needs. The CD-ROM includes an audio component for extra listening activities.

▲ **Stand Out Grammar Challenge:** Optional workbook activities provide supplemental exercises for students who desire even more contextual grammar and vocabulary practice.

◀ **Stand Out ExamView®Pro Test Bank:** Innovative test bank CD-ROM allows for pre- and post-unit quizzes. Teachers can easily print out prepared tests, or modify them to create their own customized (including computer-based) assessments.

Welcome to Our Class

GOALS

- Greet your classmates
- Say and write your name
- Say and write your phone number
- Follow classroom instructions

 **Say hello!**

GOAL ▶ Greet your classmates | **Life Skill**

 A Listen and repeat.

| hello | hi | goodbye | bye |

 B Listen.

A Listen and repeat.

Aa Bb Cc Dd Ee Ff
Gg Hh Ii Jj Kk Ll Mm
Nn Oo Pp Qq Rr Ss Tt
Uu Vv Ww Xx Yy Zz

I'm Amal.

B Listen and write.

1. I'm <u>A m a l</u>.

2. I'm __ __ __ __ __ __ __.

3. I'm __ __ __ __ __ .

4. I'm __ __ __ __.

5. I'm Mrs. __ __ __ __ __.

6. I'm __ __ __ __ __ __ .

C Write.

A a B b C c D d E e

F f G g H h I i J j K k L l M m

N n O o P p Q q R r S s T t

U u V v W w X x Y y Z z

D Write your name.

I'm _____.

E Write a classmate's name.

_____.

LESSON 3 Numbers

GOAL ▶ Say and write your phone number | **Life Skill**

  A **Listen and repeat.**

0 1 2 3 4 5 6 7 8 9 10

Chinh: (714) 555-3450

  B **Listen and circle.**

EXAMPLE: (714) 555–7682 (714) 555–0971 (714) 555–7689

1. (352) 555–6767   (352) 555–1415   (352) 555–2655

2. (808) 555–4512   (808) 555–6755   (808) 555–3456

3. (915) 555–4576   (915) 555–3466   (915) 555–3455

C **Write your phone number.**

My phone number is (__ __ __) __ __ __–__ __ __ __

LESSON 4 Class work

A Write.

listen

l _ _ _ _ _

point

p _ _ _ _

read

r _ _ _

repeat

r _ _ _ _ _

write

w _ _ _ _

  B Listen.

EXAMPLE 1:		EXAMPLE 2:	
Bubble in.	**Circle.**	**1. Bubble in.**	**2. Circle.**
○ a. listen	a. read	○ read	a. practice
○ b. point	ⓑ practice	○ repeat	b. point
● c. write	c. listen	○ write	c. write

C Practice (listen, point, read, write).

EXAMPLE:

Student A: Listen.
Student B:

UNIT 1

Personal Information

GOALS
- Use subject pronouns
- Say and write the date
- Use the verb *be*
- Say and write your address
- Fill out an application

LESSON 1 What's your name?

GOAL ▶ Use subject pronouns **Grammar**

  A Listen and point.

He is a student.

She is a student.

They are students.

I am a student.

B **Look and repeat.**

C **Write *he, she,* or *they*.**

Amal _____   Elsa and Chinh _____   Chinh _____

  **Listen.**

Chinh: My friend is here.
Elsa: He is from Vietnam, right?
Chinh: Yes, he is. I am from Vietnam, too.

E **Practice the conversation.**

F **Write classmates' names with a partner.**

Pronoun		Names
I	I am a student.	(Your name) _____
you	You are a student.	(Your partner's name) _____
he	He is a student.	_____
she	She is a student.	_____
we	We are students.	_____
they	They are students.	_____

LESSON 2 What's the date?

GOAL ▶ **Say and write the date**

A **Circle this year.**   2004   2005   2006   2007   2008

 B **Listen and point.**

September						
Sunday	**Monday**	**Tuesday**	**Wednesday**	**Thursday**	**Friday**	**Saturday**
		1	2	3	4	5
6	7	8	9	10	11	12
13	14	15	16	17	18	19
20	21	22	23	24	25	26
27	28	29	30			

 C **Number the months. Listen and point.**

January	February	March	April	May	June
1	_____	_____	_____	_____	_____

July	August	September	October	November	December
_____	_____	_____	_____	_____	_____

 D **Listen to the months and say the number. Listen again and write the months on a sheet of paper.**

E **Read and practice.**

September 15, 2004   May 7, 2005   August 26, 2005
(month day, year)   (month day, year)   (month day, year)

F **Write the date today.**   **Write your birth date.**

_____ _____, _____   _____ _____, _____
        month   day   year   month   day   year

G **Read.**

September 15, 2004   May 7, 2005   August 26, 2005
        09 / 15 / 04   05 / 07 / 05   08 / 26 / 05
(month/day/year)   (month/day/year)   (month/day/year)

H **1. Write the date today.**   **3. Write your birth date.**

_____ / _____ / _____   _____ / _____ / _____

(month /   day   / year)   (month /   day   / year)

2. Write the date tomorrow.   **4. Write your friend's birth date.**

_____ / _____ / _____   _____ / _____ / _____

(month /   day   / year)   (month /   day   / year)

What's the date today?

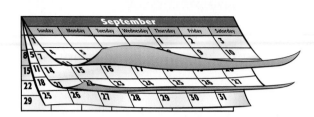

  I **Listen and write.**

Amal: What's the date today?

Chinh: It's _____.

Amal: Thanks.

J **Copy.**

Amal: *What's* _____

_____?

Chinh: _____.

Amal: _____.

K **Listen and repeat the days of the week.**

CALENDAR

_____ (this month)						
Sunday	**Monday**	**Tuesday**	**Wednesday**	**Thursday**	**Friday**	**Saturday**

L **Complete the calendar for this month.**

M **Circle today. Write the date.** _____ ____, _____ or ____ / ____ / ____

GOAL ▶ Use the verb *be*

Grammar

A **Listen and write.**

| He is single.   They are married.   They are divorced. |

He _____ .   _____ .

_____ .

B **With a partner, point at a picture in Exercise A and say *single*, *married*, or *divorced*.**

C **Listen and write.**

1. She is _____.

2. He is _____.

3. They are _____.

  D **Read.**

Be Verb			
Pronoun	**be**	**Marital status**	**Example sentence**
I	am	married	I am married.
He	is	divorced	He is divorced. (Mario is divorced.)
She		single	She is single. (Chinh is single.)
We		divorced	We are divorced.
You	are	married	You are married.
They		single	They are single.

E **Write the *be* verb.**

1. We ___are___ married.
2. They _____ divorced.
3. I _____ single.
4. He _____ married.

5. Mrs. and Mr. Adams _____ married.
6. Orlando _____ single.
7. Chinh _____ single.
8. Omar, Natalie, and Doug _____ single.

F **Read and write.**

I + am = I'm
You + are = You're
He + is = He's
She + is = She's
We + are = We're
They + are = They're

1. ___I'm___ married.
2. _____ divorced.
3. _____ single.
4. _____ divorced.
5. _____ married.
6. _____ single.

G **Read.**

Hans, are you single?   Rosa, are you single?   Pam, are you married?
Yes, I'm single.   No, I'm married.   No, I'm divorced.

H **Speak to five students.**

Name	Marital Status (Are you married?)
Hans	*single*

What's your address?

GOAL ▶ **Say and write your address**

Life Skill

A **Read.**

B **Write.**

Name: _Fawzia Ahadi_____

Street Address: _____

City: _____

State: _____

Zip Code: _____

Birth date: _____

C **Say the addresses.**

3259 Lincoln Street
51 Apple Avenue
12367 Elm Road

D **Listen and write.**

Address:

___8237___ Augustin Street

Irvine, CA 92714

Address:

_____ San Andrew Street

Irvine, CA 92618

Address:

_____ Fin Road

Irvine, CA 92603

Address:

_____ Walker Avenue

Irvine, CA 92714

E **Write.**

Name	Address
Amal	*8237 Augustin Street Irvine, CA 92714*
Elsa	
Chinh	
Orlando	

F **Read.**

Chinh: Hi, Amal. What's your address?
Amal: Hello, Chinh. My address is 8237 Augustin Street, Irvine, CA 92714.
Chinh: Thanks.

G **Write.**

Pair practice. Student A, page 12. Student B, page 11.

Student A: Hi, Chinh. What's your address?
Student B: Hello, Amal. My address is _____.
Student A: Thanks.

Student A: Hi, Elsa. What's your address?
Student B: Hello, Amal. My address is _____.
Student A: Thanks.

Student A: Hi, Orlando. What's your address?
Student B: Hello, Elsa. My address is _____.
Student A: Thanks.

H **Write.**

My name	Address

My partner	Address

I **Active Task.** Get an ID card from your school or the DMV (Department of Motor Vehicles).

GOAL ▶ **Fill out an application**

Life skill

 A **Listen and read.**

Amal: This is Matsu Tanaka. He is a student here at Locke Adult School.
Chinh: Nice to meet you.
Matsu: Nice to meet you, too.

B **Write.**
First Name: *M*_____

Last Name: _____

C **Read.**

Name: Matsu Tanaka

Birth Date: 07/02/1962

Street Address: 923 West Port Street

City: Magnolia

State: CA

Zip Code: 92808

Phone Number: (714) 555-3465

D **Write.**

Locke Adult School Application		
Last Name	First Name	Birth Date mm/dd/yyyy
Street Address		
City	State	Zip
Phone Number		

E **Listen and read.**

1. What's your name? *Matsu Tanaka*

2. What's your address? *923 West Port Street*

3. What's your birth date? *July 2, 1962*

4. What's your phone number? *(714) 555-3465*

F Write your personal information.

Locke Adult School Application		
Last Name	First Name	Birth Date mm/dd/yyyy
Street Address		
City	State	Zip
Phone Number		

G Ask your partner.

1. What's your name?
2. What's your address?

3. What's your birth date?
4. What's your phone number?

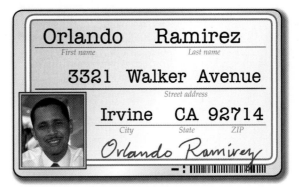

Her address is
23 San Andrew Street.

His address is
3321 Walker Avenue.

H Talk about the man on page 14.
EXAMPLE: His name is Matsu Tanaka. His birth date is . . .

I Talk to the class about your partner.
His/Her first name is . . .
His/Her last name is . . .

Review

A Read.

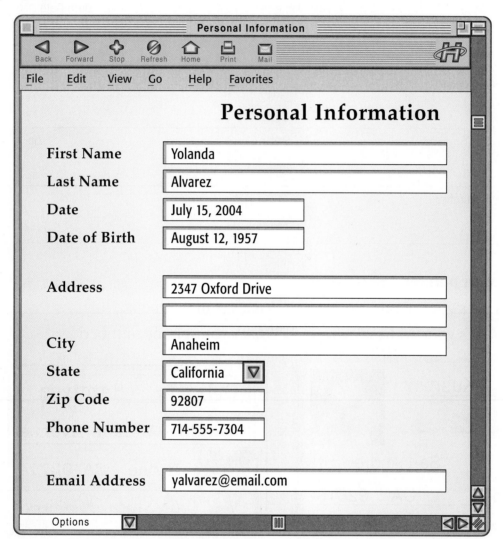

Personal Information

First Name	Yolanda
Last Name	Alvarez
Date	July 15, 2004
Date of Birth	August 12, 1957
Address	2347 Oxford Drive
City	Anaheim
State	California
Zip Code	92807
Phone Number	714-555-7304
Email Address	yalvarez@email.com

B Write.

1. What is her first name? _____

2. What is her last name? _____

3. What is her phone number? _____

4. What is her address? _____

5. What is her birth date? _____

6. What is her email address? _____

Review

C Speak to a partner. Write.

You say: What's your first name?

What's your last name?

What's your address?

What's your phone number?

What's your email address?

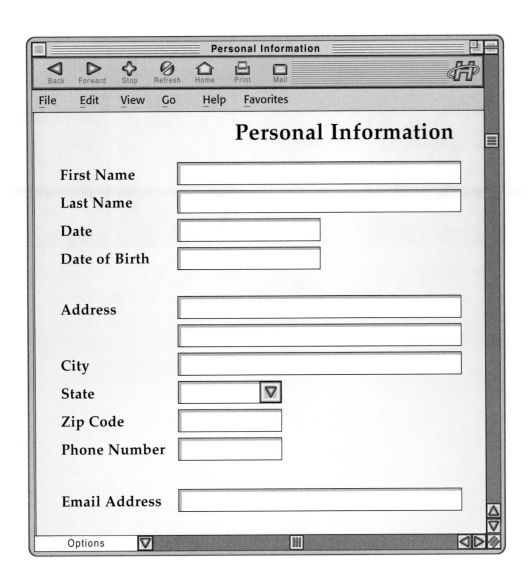

D Write.

1.

She / He / They

_____ is from Germany.

2.

She / He / They

_____ are in school.

3.

She / He / They

_____ is Ron Carter.

4.

She / He / We

_____ live in Irvine.

E Write the *be* verb.

1. She ___*is*___ a student.

2. She _____ from Japan.

3. We _____ students at Locke Adult School.

4. They _____ from Honduras.

5. I _____ in school.

6. My address _____ 27 Dawson Road.

7. You _____ my friend.

8. He _____ from the United States.

T E A M P R O J E C T

Making a class book

1. Form a team with four or five students.

   In your team, you need:

Position	Job	Student Name
Student 1 Leader	See that everyone speaks English. See that everyone participates.	
Student 2 Writer	Write information.	
Student 3 Artist	Draw pictures.	
Student 4 Spokesperson	Help group to practice presentation.	

2. Write the information for your team.
   What's your first name?
   What's your last name?
   What's your address?
   What's your phone number?
   What's your birth date?

3. Draw a picture or add a photo.

4. Make a team book.

5. Do a presentation.

6. Make a class book.

PRONUNCIATION

Listen and repeat. Can you hear the difference?

I am	I'm	you are	you're
it is	it's	we are	we're
he is	he's	she is	she's
they are	they're	what is	what's

Listen and circle.

1. I am   I'm
2. She is   She's

3. You are   You're
4. What is   What's

LEARNER LOG

Write the page number(s).

	Page Number(s)
1. I / you / he / she / we / they	_____
2. the date (March 14, 2004)	_____
3. am / are / is	_____
4. addresses	_____
5. personal information	_____

My favorite lesson in this unit is _____.

UNIT 2 Our Class

GOALS
- Identify your native country
- Talk about the weather
- Identify classroom activities
- Tell time
- Use prepositions of location

Where are you from?

GOAL ▷ Identify your native country

Life Skill

A Read and listen.

Fort Lauderdale, Florida Adult School

My name is Concepcion.

I'm from Cuba.

B Write answers.

1. What's her name? _____

2. Where is she from? _____

  C **Listen and write.**

1. She is from Cuba. _____*Concepcion*_____

2. She is from Canada. _____

3. He is from Japan. _____

4. He is from Senegal. _____

5. He is from Fort Lauderdale, Florida. _____

D **Practice.**

EXAMPLE: **A:** Where is <u>Concepcion</u> from?
         B: She's from <u>Cuba</u>.

E   **Complete.**

_____ is from Cuba.

She lives in _____.

F   **Listen and practice.**

Mr. Jackson: Hi, <u>Concepcion</u>. Where are you from?
Concepcion: I'm from <u>Cuba</u>.
Mr. Jackson: Where do you live?
Concepcion: I live in <u>Fort Lauderdale, Florida</u>.

G   **Write about yourself.**

I'm from _____.

I live in _____.

H   **Practice and write. Ask your classmates.**

You: Hi, _____. Where are you from?

Classmate: I'm from _____.

You: Where do you live?

Classmate: I live in _____.

	Name (What's your name?)	Country (Where are you from?)	Current City (Where do you live?)
1.			
2.			
3.			
4.			
5.			
6.			
7.			
8.			

GOAL ▶ **Talk about the weather**

 A **Listen and repeat.**

| windy | cloudy | foggy | rainy | cold | hot | sunny |

 B **Listen and write.**

Havana, Cuba

hot, sunny

Montreal, Canada

_____

Tokyo, Japan

_____

Lisbon, Portugal

_____

Patagonia, Chile

_____

Mombasa, Kenya

_____

C **Read.**

A: How's the weather in <u>Havana, Cuba</u> today?

B: It's <u>hot and sunny</u>.

D **Practice new conversations.**

Havana, Cuba

London, England

Capetown, South Africa

Moscow, Russia

Vancouver, Canada

Ensenada, Mexico

  E **Listen and write.**

1. It's _____*hot*_____ today.

2. It's _____ today.

3. It's _____ today.

4. It's _____ today.

F What is the rainfall in each country?

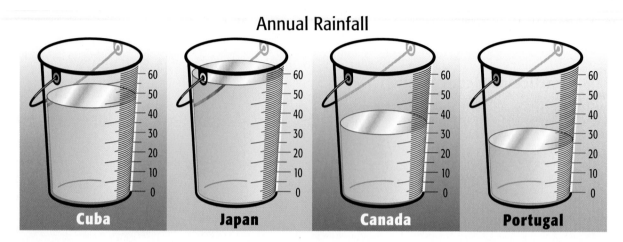

Annual Rainfall

Cuba   Japan   Canada   Portugal

G Write the countries on the graph.

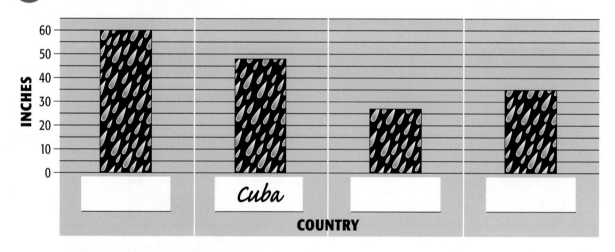

INCHES

Cuba

COUNTRY

annual = every year

H How is the weather today in your city? Write the answer.

It's _____.

I **Active Task:** Go to the Internet or look in the newspaper. How is the weather in your country today?

What are you doing?

GOAL ▶ **Identify classroom activities**

A Listen and point.

B Write the name of the student.

1. listen _____

2. read _____

3. write _____

4. talk _____

C Write and match.

1.

   ___pen___

2.

   _____

3.

   _____

4.

   _____

listen

write

read

write

D Study.

Raise your hand.   Stand up.   Sit down.

E Practice. Say the word. Do the action.

| talk | read | stand up | write |
| raise your hand | sit down | listen | |

Write.

talk	read	stand
write	sit	listen

1. _____ *read, listen* _____

_____

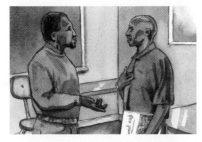

2. _____

_____

3. _____

_____

4. _____

_____

Point and practice.

A: (point to Concepcion)
B: Read and listen.

GOAL ▶ **Tell time**

A **Read and listen.**

Shiro's Schedule

MONDAY	
9:00 A.M.	English Class
12:00 P.M.	Lunch
1:00 P.M.	Pronunciation Class
4:00 P.M.	Work

B **Write.**

1. What time is English class? _____*It's at 9:00 A.M.*_____

2. What time is lunch? _____

3. What time is pronunciation class? _____

4. What time is work? _____

C What time is it now? Write.

1.

It's ___3:00___.

2.

It's _____.

3.

It's _____.

4.

It's _____.

D What time is it now? Bubble in and write.

1.

○ 3:30
○ 4:30

It's ___3:30___.

2.

○ 5:00
○ 5:30

It's _____.

3.

○ 5:00
○ 7:30

It's _____.

4.

○ 10:30
○ 10:00

It's _____.

5.

○ 10:30
○ 11:30

It's _____.

6.

○ 6:30
○ 8:30

It's _____.

7.

○ 1:30
○ 2:30

It's _____.

E Point and practice.

EXAMPLE: **A:** (Point to #3 in Exercise D.) What time is it?
B: It's 7:30.

F **Listen and write.**

Julie's Schedule	
Monday	
_____9:00_____	English class
_____	Work
_____	Lunch
_____	Bedtime

 G **Listen and read.**

Concepcion: What time is English class?
Mr. Jackson: It's at 9:00.
Concepcion: What time is it now?
Mr. Jackson: It's 7:30.

> What time is English class?
> It's *at* 9:00.
> What time is it now?
> It's ~~at~~ 7:30.

H **Practice.**

A: What time is _____?

B: It's _____.

A: What time is it now?

B: It's _____.

I **Write your schedule.**

5 Where is the pencil sharpener?

GOAL ▶ Use prepositions of location

Grammar

A Listen and repeat. Point to the picture.

| trash can | file cabinets | board | bookcase | plant | door |

B Write these words in the picture—*desk, tables, computers, chairs,* and *books*.

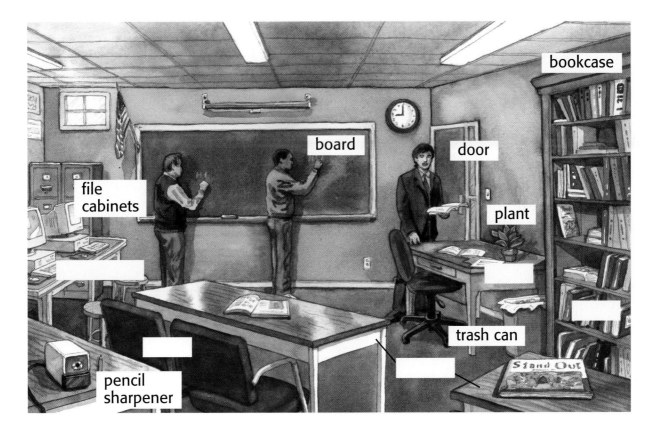

C Listen and point.

Read.

Where is the teacher?
next to the door

Where is the plant?
on the desk

Where is the trash can?
between the desk and the bookcase

 Read.

Where are the file cabinets?
in back of the computers

Where are the students?
in front of the board

Where are the books?
in the bookcase

 Practice (teacher, plant, trash can, file cabinets, students, books).
A: (Look at page 34.) Where is the teacher?
B: (Look at page 33.) next to the door
B: (Look at page 34.) Where are the file cabinets?
A: (Look at page 33.) in back of the computers

G In groups, draw your classroom.

H Write.

1. Where is the teacher's desk? _____

2. Where is the trash can? _____

3. Where is the board? _____

4. Where are the books? _____

5. Where are the file cabinets? _____

6. Where are the chairs? _____

7. Where is the clock? _____

8. Where are the tables? _____

A **Read.**

Choi Soon Young
Seoul, Korea

Irma Perez
Guadalajara, Mexico

Christine Brideau
Roanne, France

Binh Duong
Lao Cai, Vietnam

B **Write.**

1. Where is Choi Soon from?

   He is from _____.

2. Where is Christine from?

   _____.

3. Where is Irma from?

   _____.

4. Where is Binh from?

   _____.

C **Practice.**

EXAMPLE: Where is Choi Soon from?
He's from Seoul, Korea.

Review

D Read. Talk about the weather and the time in each place.

Seoul, Korea

Guadalajara, Mexico

Roanne, France

Lao Cai, Vietnam

 E Write.

How's the weather in Korea?   _It's rainy in Korea._

What time is it?   _It's 8:00._

How's the weather in France?   _____

What time is it?   _____

How's the weather in Mexico?   _____

What time is it?   _____

How's the weather in Vietnam?   _____

What time is it?   _____

F Write.

_It's 3:30._ _____   _____   _____

G Match. Draw a line.

1.

2.

a. Listen.

b. Write.

3.

c. Talk.

d. Read.

4.

H Write.

_in_ _____   _____   _____

T E A M
P R O J E C T

Making a display

1. Form a team with four or five students.

   In your team, you need:

Position	Job	Student Name
Student 1 Leader	See that everyone speaks English. See that everyone participates.	
Student 2 Artist	Arrange a display with help from the team.	
Student 3 Writer	Help team members write.	
Student 4 Spokesperson	Prepare a presentation.	

2. Draw information about yourself on the team sheet of paper.

   Draw a picture of yourself.

   Draw a map of your country.

   Draw a clock with the time in your country.

   Draw the weather in your country.

3. Present your work to the class.

PRONUNCIATION

Listen to the vowel sound in these words. Underline the words with a long /a/ sound. Circle the words with a short /e/ sound. Then listen again and repeat.

<u>name</u>   (ten)   May   desk   they

eight   weather   next   lane   seven

LEARNER LOG

Write the page number(s).

	Page Number(s)
1. Identify your country	_____
2. weather	_____
3. read, write, talk, listen	_____
4. time	_____
5. in / on / next to / between	_____

My favorite lesson in this unit is _____.

UNIT 3 Food

GOALS
- Identify foods
- Express hunger
- Use singular and plural nouns
- Make a shopping list
- Express preferences

LESSON 1 Let's eat!

GOAL ▶ Identify foods	*Vocabulary*

  A Listen.

What's the name of the school?
Where are they?

  B Listen again.

Andre: The food looks good!
Silvina: Yes, it does.
Andre: What are you eating?
Silvina: A turkey sandwich.

C **Listen and point.**

a. milk	f. bread	k. apples
b. water	g. cheese	l. oranges
c. eggs	h. turkey	m. potatoes
d. chicken	i. tomatoes	n. mayonnaise
e. bananas	j. lettuce	o. butter

D **Read and write the words.**

1. The _____ is next to the water.

2. The _____ is between the bread and the cheese.

3. The _____ are next to the apples.

Practice.

EXAMPLE:

A: What is next to the <u>milk</u>?

B: The <u>water</u>.

 In a group, write words from Exercise C.

Breakfast	Lunch	Dinner
milk	*water*	*milk*

 What do you eat? Write.

Breakfast	Lunch	Dinner

GOAL ▶ Express hunger | *Life Skill*

A Look at the picture.

Saul and Chen are studying English.
What's for dinner?

B Listen and read.

Saul: I'm hungry.
Chen: Me, too.
Saul: What's for dinner?
Chen: <u>Chicken and vegetables</u>.

C Practice Exercise B.

What's for dinner?

chicken sandwiches | hamburgers | tacos and chips | rice and
and fruit | and fries | | vegetables

D **Read.**

Saul is hungry. He is not thirsty.   Chen is thirsty. He is not hungry.

be Verb			
Pronoun	***be***		**Example sentence**
I	am (not)		I am hungry. I'm not thirsty.
He	is (not)	hungry	He is hungry. He's not thirsty.
She		very hungry	She is thirsty. She's not hungry.
We		thirsty	We are thirsty. We're not hungry.
You	are (not)		You are hungry. You're not thirsty.
They			They are hungry. They're not thirsty.

E **Write. Follow the example sentences in the chart.**

EXAMPLE: Edgar ___*is*___ hungry. *He's not thirsty.*

1. Roselia and Thanh _____ thirsty.

   _____

2. We _____ very hungry.

   _____

3. She _____ not hungry.

   _____

4. I _____ thirsty.

   _____

5. You _____ not hungry.

   _____

F **Read and listen.**

carrots

oranges

apples

milk

chips

water

cookies

G **Listen and write the snack.**

1. _____*carrots*_____

2. _____

3. _____

4. _____

H **Practice.**

A: I'm hungry.

B: What's good?

A: How about <u>carrots</u>?

B: Great!

I **What snacks do you eat? Write.**

_____

_____

_____

Let's have spaghetti.

GOAL ▶ **Use singular and plural nouns**

A **Read the ingredients.**

Spaghetti and Meatballs

Serves 6 people

Ingredients:

2 jars of tomato sauce	2 pounds of ground beef
2 eggs	salt
1 onion	pepper
1 package of spaghetti	

...apidly boiling water, cook the pasta according to the package directions. Combine
...in another bowl, mix the eggs with the chopped onion in a large bowl. Add
...dd the beef and mix well. Shape into 48 equal
...° for 15 minutes. Add meatballs
...rve

B **Write.**

1. How many jars of tomato sauce? _____*2 jars*_____

2. How many eggs? _____

3. How many onions? _____

4. How many packages of spaghetti? _____

5. How many pounds of ground beef? _____

C Read the chart and listen. Repeat.

Singular Form	Plural Form
jar 	jars 
egg 	eggs 
onion 	onions 
package 	packages 
pound 	pounds 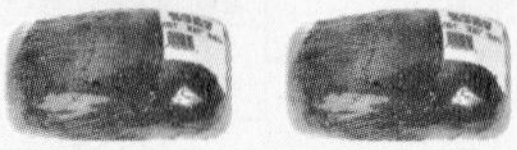

Exceptions

potato	potato<u>es</u>
tomato	tomato<u>es</u>
sandwich	sandwich<u>es</u>

D Write the plural forms.

Fruit		Vegetables	
apple	*apples*	carrot	
orange		tomato	
banana		potato	
pear 		green pepper 	

E **Write the words.**

  _____eggs_____   _____

  _____   _____

  _____   _____

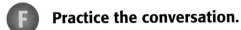 _____   _____

F **Practice the conversation.**

A: What are the ingredients?
B: <u>Two eggs and one onion</u>.

G **Make a fruit salad. What do you need?**

		Fruit Salad		Serves 6 people
Ingredients:	_1_	banana	___	_____
	_2_	apple**s**	___	_____
	___	pear	___	_____
	___	orange	___	_____

LESSON **4** **What's for dinner?**

GOAL ▶ **Make a shopping list** **Life Skill**

 A **Listen and point.**

B **Write the words on the correct shopping lists.**

Shopping List	Shopping List	Shopping List	Shopping List
Meat and Fish	Vegetables	Fruit	Dairy
1.	1.	1.	1.
2.	2.	2.	2.
3.	3.	3.	3.
4.	4.	4.	
	5.	5.	

C **Do you know more food words? Add them to the shopping list.**

D **Read Amadeo's shopping list.**

Shopping List

apples	tomatoes
water	chicken
milk	eggs
carrots	chips
cheese	

E **What does Amadeo want? Circle the items.**

oranges

apples

eggs

potatoes

cheese

broccoli

 F **What does Yoshi want? Listen and write.**

Shopping List	
oranges	

G **Write.**

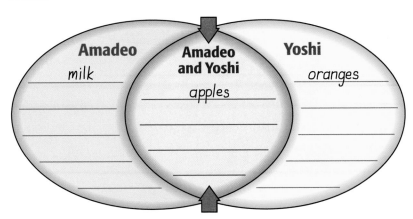

Amadeo
milk

Amadeo and Yoshi
apples

Yoshi
oranges

H **What do you want?**
Make a list.

I **What does your partner want?**
Write your partner's list.

What do you want?

J **Write.**

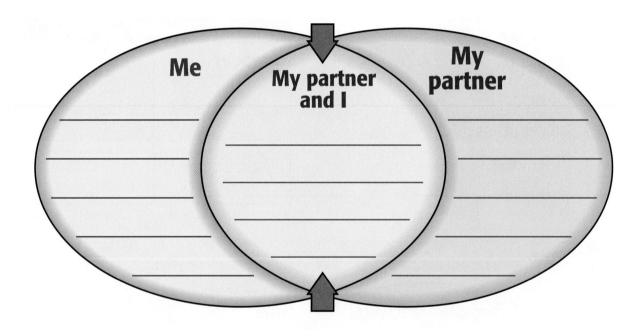

K **Active Task:** Make a shopping list and go to the store.

GOAL ▶ **Express preferences**　　　　　　　*Life Skill*

A　**Circle the foods you like to eat. Then listen and repeat.**

Desserts

cake　　　　pie　　　　ice cream　　　　fruit
　　　　　　　　　　　　　cone

sundae　　　　cookies　　　　chocolate　　　　candy

B　**Listen. Write what Maria likes.**

Maria likes _____.

Maria likes _____.

Maria likes _____.

C　**Listen and point to the desserts in Exercise A.**

D **Read the chart.**

Simple Present		
Pronoun	**Verb**	**Example sentence**
I, you, we, they	**like**	I like ice cream.
he, she, it	**likes**	She likes chocolate.

E **Write like or likes.**

1. Maria ____likes____ ice cream cones.

2. I _____ apple pie.

3. You _____ sundaes.

4. They _____ cookies.

5. We _____ fruit.

6. He _____ cake.

7. We _____ chocolate.

8. She _____ candy.

F **Write about the pictures.**

1. _He likes cookies._

2. _____

3. _____

G **Write. What do you like?**

I like _____.

I _____.

_____

H **Complete the chart.**

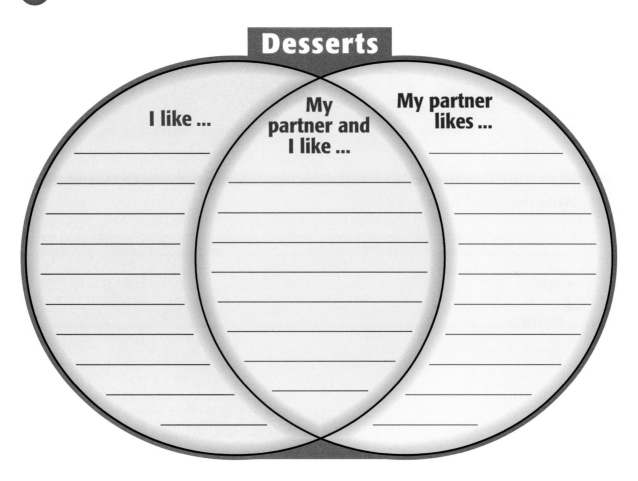

Desserts

I like ...

My partner and I like ...

My partner likes ...

Review

A Write the food words.

_____ _____ _____ _____ _____

_____ _____ _____ _____ _____

B Write the plural food words.

Singular	Plural
apple	_____
orange	_____
chicken	_____
banana	_____
cookie	_____
egg	_____
chip	_____
potato	_____
tomato	_____
carrot	_____

C **Write *am, is,* or *are*.**

1. Maria _____ thirsty.

2. Kim and David _____ not hungry.

3. Lan and Mai _____ hungry.

4. Rafael _____ not thirsty.

5. Colby _____ hungry.

6. I _____.

D **Write sentences.**

EXAMPLE: Eric is hungry. ___*He's not thirsty.*___

1. Maria is thirsty._____

2. Saul and Chen are hungry. _____

3. I am thirsty. _____

E **Write *like* or *likes*.**

1. Chrissy _____ hamburgers.

2. Antonio and Bibi _____ tacos.

3. Laura _____ vegetables.

4. Rosie and I _____ rice.

5. Mr. Hoa _____ fish and chicken.

6. I _____.

F Talk to two people.

What food do you want?

Partner 1   Partner 2

Shopping List		Shopping List	

G Read lists. Write.

Singular Foods	Plural Foods

TEAM PROJECT

Making a shopping list

1. Form a team with four or five students.
   In your team, you need:

Position	Job	Student Name
Student 1 Leader	See that everyone speaks English. See that everyone participates.	
Student 2 Artist	Draw pictures of food for the shopping list with help from the team.	
Student 3 Writer	Write food names.	
Student 4 Spokesperson	Prepare a presentation.	

2. You are a family. What is your last name?

3. Make a shopping list with food from this unit.

4. Draw pictures of the food on your list.

5. Present your list to the class.

PRONUNCIATION

Listen to the final 's' sound in these words. Can you hear the difference?

/s/	/z/	/ɪz/
carrots	apples	oranges
chips	eggs	packages
snacks	tomatoes	dishes

Listen. Circle the last sound you hear.

1. /s/ /z/ /ɪz/   3. /s/ /z/ /ɪz/
2. /s/ /z/ /ɪz/   4. /s/ /z/ /ɪz/

LEARNER LOG

Write the page number(s).

	Page Number(s)
1. Identify foods	_____
2. I'm hungry.	_____
3. plurals	_____
4. I want. / He wants.	_____
5. I like. / He likes.	_____

My favorite lesson in this unit is _____.

UNIT 4

Clothing

GOALS
- Identify types of clothing
- Identify colors and describe clothing
- Identify prices and count money
- Form questions
- Write checks

LESSON 1 — What's on sale?

GOAL ▶ Identify types of clothing   *Vocabulary*

What's the name of the store?
What does Maria want?

  A **Listen.**

Salesperson: May I help you?
Maria: Yes, I want this shirt and this sweater, please.

B Read and listen.

a blouse	a coat	a dress	shorts	a sweater
pants	a shirt	shoes	socks	

C Write the words under the pictures.

shoes _____ _____ _____

_____ _____ _____ _____ _____

_a_ dress = one dress = 1 dress	a shoe
two dresses = 2 dresses	a pair of shoes

D Write.

Singular	Plural
a shirt	_shirts_
a dress	
a blouse	
a sweater	
a coat	
a shoe	

E **What's in the ad?**

F **Read and practice.**

Salesperson: Can I help you?
Customer: What's on sale?
Salesperson: Today, <u>shirts</u> are on sale.
Customer: Great!

G **Listen. What is in Maria's closet?**

Maria's Closet
_____3 dresses_____
1 pair of s_____
1 bl_____
2 c_____
4 pairs of p_____

H **Write. What's in your closet?**

My Closet

_____
_____
_____
_____

2 What color do you like?

| GOAL ▶ Identify colors and describe clothing | *Vocabulary* |

A Talk about the picture with your teacher.

What is Yusuf doing?
What color shirt do you like for Yusuf?

  B Listen and read.

Salesperson: Can I help you?
Yusuf: Yes, I want a shirt.
Salesperson: What color do you like—white, blue, or red?
Yusuf: I don't know, maybe blue.

C **Listen and repeat.**

red   yellow   blue   green   white   black

S = small   M = medium   L = large   XL = extra large

blue shirt	~~shirt blue~~
(correct)	(not correct)

D **Listen and point.**

E **Look at Exercise D. Complete the chart.**

Adel's Inventory List			
Quantity (How many?)	**Item**	**Size**	**Color**
3	shirt	S	
2	shirt	M	
1	shirt	L	
2	shirt	XL	

Read.

Singular	Plural
There **is** one white shirt.	There **are** two green shirts.

G **Read and practice. Use the information in Exercise E.**

How many <u>white shirts</u> are there?

There <u>is one</u>.

H **Write a class inventory.**

My Class Inventory List		
Quantity (How many?)	Item	Color

I **Activity Task:** Go home and write an inventory of your closet.

LESSON 3 That's $5.00.

GOAL ▶ **Identify prices and count money**

 A Listen and read the cash registers.

1.

2.

3.

B Bubble in the number from Exercise A.

	1	2	3
one dollar	○	○	○

	1	2	3
ten dollars and forty-one cents	○	○	○

	1	2	3
six dollars and twenty-five cents	○	○	○

C Listen and read.

a dollar bill	a quarter	a dime	a nickel	a penny
$1.00	$.25	$.10	$.05	$.01

D Draw a line.

1.

a.

2.

b.

3.

c.

E Listen and write the price.

1.   *$32.50*

2.   _____

3.   _____

4.   _____

5.   _____

6.   _____

F Write the prices from Exercise E.

Adel's Clothing

shirt	_____
shoes	_____
Total	**$68.50**

CUSTOMER COPY

Adel's Clothing

dress	_____
shorts	_____
blouse	_____
Total	**$123.00**

CUSTOMER COPY

Adel's Clothing

| pants | $32.50 |
| **Total** | **$32.50** |

CUSTOMER COPY

G Write a receipt. Buy three items.

Adel's Clothing

	_____
	_____
	_____
Total	

CUSTOMER COPY

A Read, listen, and write.

B Write.

1. How much are the shirts?   *$22.50*

2. How much are the dresses?   _____

3. How much are the shoes?   _____

4. How much are the blouses?   _____

C Read.

Forming Questions	
Question	**Answer**
How much <u>is</u> the shirt?	**It's** $22.50.
How much <u>are</u> the shirts?	**They** <u>are</u> $22.50 each.
How many shirts do you want?	I want one shirt.
How many shoes do you want?	I want two **pairs** of shoes.

D Practice answering questions.

A: Can I help you?

B: Yes. I want some <u>shirts</u>.

A: How many shirts do you want?

B: I want two shirts. How much are they?

A: They are <u>$22.50</u> each.

E Practice taking orders from four students. Write. (See the ad on page 70.)

Name	Quantity (How many?)	Product	Price (Each item)	Total
Yusuf	*2*	*shirts*	*$22.50*	*$45.00*

F Write the questions.

Question: *How much is the shirt?*

Answer: $22.50

Question: _____

Answer: Two pairs of shoes.

Question: _____

Answer: $33.00

Question: _____

Answer: Three blouses.

G In a group, use the pictures to make an ad (see Exercise A) and practice a conversation (see Exercise D).

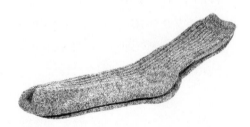

LESSON 5 Do you take checks?

GOAL ▶ Write checks *Life Skill*

 A **Talk about the picture.**

What is Ivan doing?
What is in his hand?

 B **Listen.**

Salesperson: Can I help you?

Ivan: Yes, I'm ready.

Salesperson: OK, one pair of shoes. That's $34.50.

Ivan: Do you take checks?

Salesperson: Of course!

C **Read the check.**

IVAN BORICOV
8233 HENDERSON STREET
NEW YORK CITY, NY 10012

1025

DATE: *March 13, 2005*

PAY TO THE
ORDER OF *Adel's Clothing Emporium* | $ *34.50*

thirty-four and ⁵⁰⁄₁₀₀ ～～～ DOLLARS 🔒

NATIONBANK

Ivan Boricov

MEMO *Shoes*

MP

⑆0009345 AB876543 ⑈01025

 D **Listen and write the *date, dollar amount,* and *memo*.**

IVAN BORICOV
8233 HENDERSON STREET
NEW YORK CITY, NY 10012

1026

DATE:

PAY TO THE
ORDER OF *Adel's Clothing Emporium* | $

fifty-five and ⁵⁰⁄₁₀₀ ～～～ DOLLARS 🔒

NATIONBANK

Ivan Boricov

MEMO

MP

⑆0009345 AB876543 ⑈01026

E Review numbers.

$20	**twenty** dollars	$21	**twenty-one** dollars
$30	**thirty** dollars	$32	**thirty-two** dollars
$40	**forty** dollars	$43	**forty-three** dollars
$50	**fifty** dollars	$54	**fifty-four** dollars
$60	**sixty** dollars	$65	**sixty-five** dollars
$70	**seventy** dollars	$76	**seventy-six** dollars
$80	**eighty** dollars	$87	**eighty-seven** dollars
$90	**ninety** dollars	$98	**ninety-eight** dollars

F Write.

Pay to the order of
Adel's Clothing Emporium   **$22.00**
Twenty-two and $^{00}/_{100}$ **Dollars**

Pay to the order of
Adel's Clothing Emporium   **$36.00**
_____   **Dollars**

Pay to the order of
Adel's Clothing Emporium   **$68.00**
_____   **Dollars**

Pay to the order of
Adel's Clothing Emporium   **$57.00**
_____   **Dollars**

G Copy the check from Exercise D. Write a check to Adel's Clothing Emporium for two items from page 70.

Review

A Write the words.

B Read and write in the chart.

1. We need three blue shirts. They are $18.59 each.

2. We need five green sweaters. They are $22.50 each.

3. We need one pair of black shoes. They are $33.00 each.

4. We need two red coats. They are $85.00 each.

	Adel's Clothing			
	Quantity (How many?)	Item	Color	Total Price
1.	3	shirt	blue	$55.77
2.				$112.50
3.				$33.00
4.				$170.00

C Write the totals.

① Adel's Clothing
2 shirts $34.50
Total $69.00
CUSTOMER COPY

② Adel's Clothing
1 blouse $22.50
Total
CUSTOMER COPY

③ Adel's Clothing
2 sweaters $28.45
Total
CUSTOMER COPY

④ Adel's Clothing
4 dresses $33.00
Total
CUSTOMER COPY

⑤ Adel's Clothing
3 shirts $51.25
Total
CUSTOMER COPY

⑥ Adel's Clothing
2 sweaters $56.90
Total
CUSTOMER COPY

D What money do you need for Exercise C? Fill in the chart.

	Total	$20 bills	$10 bills	$5 bills	$1 bills	quarters	dimes	nickels	pennies
1.									
2.	$22.50	1			2	2			
3.									
4.									
5.									
6.									

E Read the ad.

F Write a check for two of the items in Exercise E.

		1222
		Date: _____
Pay to the order of	_____	$ _____
	_____	**Dollars**
Nation Bank		
Memo _____	_____	

Opening a clothing store

1. Form a team with four or five students.

   In your team, you need:

Position	Job	Student Name
Student 1 Leader	See that everyone speaks English. See that everyone participates.	
Student 2 Artist	Make an ad for clothing.	
Student 3 Writer	Make an inventory list.	
Student 4 Spokesperson	Prepare a presentation.	

2. Open a store. What is the name?

3. Make an ad. (Look at pages 63 and 70.)

4. Write an inventory list.

5. Present your store to the class.

PRONUNCIATION

Listen to the /b/ and /p/ sounds in these words. Can you hear the difference? Listen and repeat.

pear   bear   bay   pay   bill pill   buy   pie

Listen and write *b* or *p*.

1. ___ear   3. ___ay
2. ___ox   4. ___ill

LEARNER LOG

Write the page number(s).

<table>
<tr><td></td><td>Page Number(s)</td></tr>
<tr><td>1. Identify clothing</td><td>_____</td></tr>
<tr><td>2. colors, sizes</td><td>_____</td></tr>
<tr><td>3. dollars, quarters, nickels</td><td>_____</td></tr>
<tr><td>4. How much / How many</td><td>_____</td></tr>
<tr><td>5. Write checks</td><td>_____</td></tr>
</table>

My favorite lesson in this unit is _____.

Our Community

GOALS

- Identify and ask about locations
- Talk about housing
- Identify types of transportation
- Use the simple present
- Give and follow directions

LESSON 1 Where we live

GOAL ▶ Identify and ask about locations   *Vocabulary*

 A **Listen and point.**

1.    2.    3.

4.    5.

 B **Listen and write the number.**

_____ pharmacy   *1* supermarket   _____ clothing store

_____ shoe store   _____ video store

C Listen and point to the sign.

D Write.

Place to sleep	Places to eat	Places to buy (stores)
		clothing store

Read.

Question	Answer
Where do you live?	**in** New York
Where do you buy clothing?	**at** a clothing store
Where do you buy food?	**at** a supermarket

F **Write and practice with a partner.**

Where do you eat? _____.

Where do you buy shoes? _____.

Where do you buy medicine? _____.

Where do you buy clothing? _____.

G **Practice with a partner.**

A: Peter, where do you buy food?
B: At <u>Jack's Supermarket</u>
A: Where do you eat?
B: At <u>Rudolfo's Mexican Café</u>

H **Talk about your community. Write.**

Name	Places
Peter	*Jack's Supermarket, Rudolfo's Mexican Café*

GOAL ▶ **Talk about housing**

A Talk about the map.

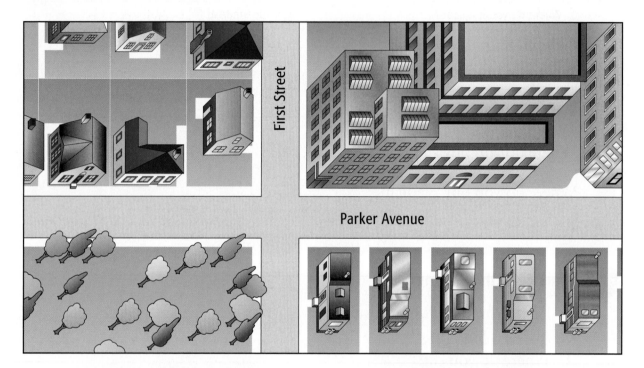

First Street

Parker Avenue

| I live **on** First Street. |
| I live **in** a house. |

| **a** house |
| **a** mobile home |
| **an** <u>a</u>partment |

B Listen and practice.

A: Where do you live?
B: I live on First Street.
A: Do you live in a house or an apartment?
B: I live in a house.

C Read.

FOR SALE 3-bedroom house 3114 Parker Ave.	**FOR SALE** 1-bedroom condominium **212 First Street**	★**FOR RENT**★ 2-bedroom apartment 3232 Parker Ave.

D Bubble in the correct answer.

1. What home is on 212 First Street?

   ○ the house

   ○ the apartment

   ○ the condominium

2. What home is for sale?

   ○ the apartment

   ○ only the condominium

   ○ the house and the condominium

3. What home is 1-bedroom?

   ○ only the apartment

   ○ only the house

   ○ the condominium

4. What home is for rent?

   ○ only the apartment

   ○ only the house

   ○ the house and the apartment

E **Listen and point.**

I'm Chen.
I'm from China.
I live in a house.
I live on First Street in
Alpine City.

I'm Latifa.
I'm from Saudi Arabia.
I live in an apartment
in Casper Town
on Parker Avenue.

I'm Natalia.
I'm from Guatemala.
I live in a condominium
on First Street.

F **Practice the conversation.**

Chen: Hi, I'm Chen.

Latifa: Nice to meet you, Chen. I'm Latifa.

Chen: Where do you live?

Latifa: I live in Casper Town.

Chen: Do you live in an apartment, a condominium, or a house?

Latifa: I live in an apartment.

G **Write a conversation.**

Latifa: <u>*Hi, I'm Latifa.*</u>

Natalia: <u>*Nice to meet you, Latifa. I'm Natalia.*</u>

Latifa: _____

Natalia: _____

Latifa: _____

Natalia: _____

H **Write and practice a conversation about you and a partner.**

GOAL ▶ **Identify types of transportation**   *Vocabulary*

A **Look at the map. How far is it from Casper Town to Alpine City?**

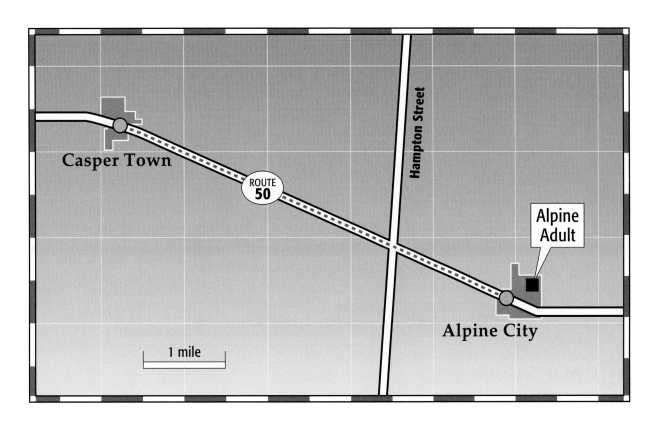

Casper Town

ROUTE **50**

Hampton Street

Alpine Adult

Alpine City

1 mile

B **Listen and read.**

Chen: Do you drive to school?
Latifa: No, I don't. I take the bus.
Chen: How much is it?
Latifa: It's 75 cents.

C   **Read the bar graph.**

Transportation Costs to Alpine City

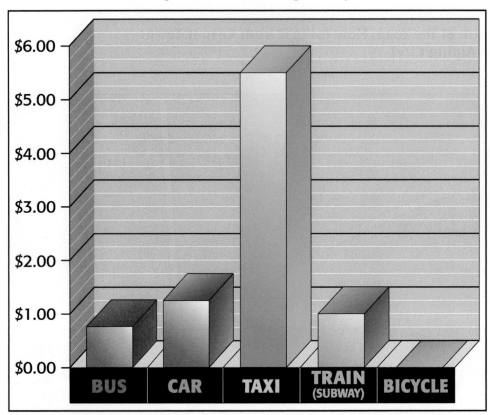

| | BUS | CAR | TAXI | TRAIN (SUBWAY) | BICYCLE |

D   **Write the words.**

   *bus*

E **Read.**

drive a car	take a bus
ride a bike	take a train
walk	take a taxi

F **Practice the conversation.**

Latifa: How do you come to school?
Natalia: I <u>drive</u>.
Latifa: How much is it?
Natalia: It's <u>$1.25</u>.

It's $0.00 = It's free.

G **Practice new conversations. Use other types of transportation.**

H **Complete the chart about four students.**

Name	Transportation (How do you come to school?)	Cost (How much is it?)
Chen	*drive*	*$.25*

I **Talk about your chart to the class.**

EXAMPLE: Chen drives to school. It costs 25 cents.

J **Active Task:** How much is the bus from your home to school? _____

GOAL ▶ Use the simple present | *Grammar*

 A **Listen and write.**

I am James.
I'm from the U.S.
I live in a house.
I take the _____ to school.

I am Nga.
I'm from Vietnam.
I live in a house.
I _____ a bicycle to school.

I am Carina.
I'm from Cuba.
I live in an
_____.
I drive to school.

 B **Write.**

Name	Country	Housing	Transportation
James			
Nga			
Carina			

C Read.

Simple Present		
Subject	**Verb**	**Example sentence**
I	live	I live in Mexico.
he, she, it	walks	He walks to school.
		She drives a car.
		It costs two dollars.
we, you, they	take	We take the bus.
		You ride a bicycle.
		They take the train.

D Write about James, Nga, and Carina.

1. James _____*lives*_____ in a house.

2. He _____ the bus to school.

3. Carina _____ in an apartment.

4. She _____ to school.

5. Nga _____ in a house.

6. She _____ a bicycle to school.

7. James and Nga _____ in a house.

E Write about Leslie and Briana.

1. Leslie and Briana _____ in Turkey.

2. Leslie _____ the bus to work every day.

3. Briana _____ a car to work.

4. They _____ in a house.

F   **Read.**

Simple Present: *be* Verb		
Pronoun	***be* verb**	**Example sentence**
I	am	I am Nga.
he, she, it,	is	She is from China.
we, you, they	are	They are married.

G   **Read the chart.**

Name	Country	Housing	Transportation to school
Karen	U.S.A.	house	bus
Lidia	U.S.A.	apartment	train
Sang	China	condominium	bus

H   **Write.**

1. Karen and Lidia _____*are*_____ (be) from the U.S.A.

2. Karen _____ (live) in a house.

3. She _____ (take) the bus.

4. Sang _____ (be) from China.

5. He _____ (live) in a condominium.

6. Karen and Sang _____ (take) the bus.

I   **Answer the questions.**

1. **What's your name?**

   My name _____.

2. **Where are you from?**

   I _____ from _____.

3. **Do you live in a house?**

   I _____ in a(n) _____.

4. **How do you come to school?**

   I _____ to school.

Where's the store?

GOAL ▶ **Give and follow directions**   **Life Skill**

A **Talk about the map of Alpine City.**

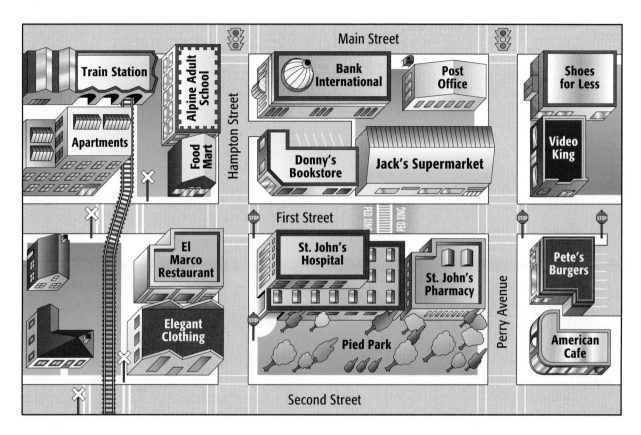

B **Learn the new words.**

bank	post office	hospital

C **Match. Draw a line.**

1. Where is the adult school?   a. It's on Perry Avenue next to Shoes for Less.

2. Where is the video store?   b. It's on First Street next to the supermarket.

3. Where is the bookstore?   c. It's on Main Street next to the bank.

4. Where is the post office?   d. It's on Hampton Street next to Food Mart.

D **Listen and repeat.**

| stop | go straight | turn right | turn left |

E **Write the correct words.**

_____ _____ _____ _____

F **Read the map.**

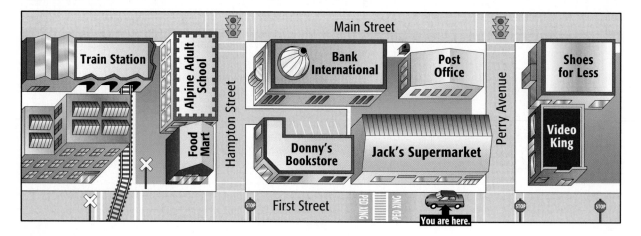

G **Where is the adult achool? Write the sentences.**

↑ on First Street. *Go straight on First Street.* _____

↱ on Hampton Street. _____

🛑 at the adult school. _____

H **Write directions from the shoe store to the bookstore, the bank, and the train station.**

I **Listen and read.**

Carina: Excuse me, where's American Café?
Nga: It's on Perry Avenue.
Carina: Can you give me directions?
Nga: Yes. Go straight on First Street. Turn right on Perry Avenue.
      It's next to Pete's Burgers.

J **Listen and follow the directions. Draw a line.**

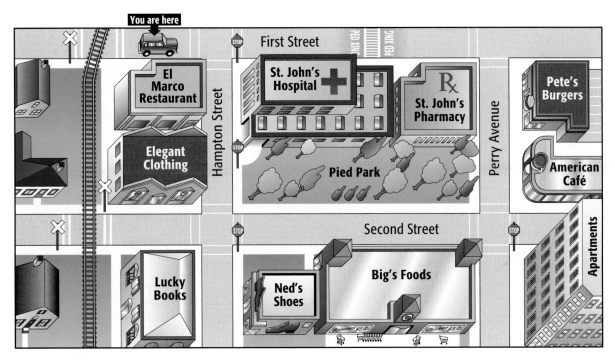

K **Write three stores in your community.**

_____

_____

_____

L **Write directions to one store from your school.**

_____

_____

_____

Review

A. Write the correct number.

_____ apartment

_____ bank

_____ bus

_1_ car

_____ hospital

_____ house

_____ pharmacy

_____ stop

_____ supermarket

_____ taxi

_____ train

_____ turn left

1.

2.

3.

4.

5.

6.

7.

8.

9.

10.

11.

12.

B. Practice with a partner.

1. Where do you live?
2. Where do you buy clothing?
3. Where do you buy shoes?
4. Where do you eat?

I'm Aki.
I'm from Japan.
I live in an apartment.
I live in New York on 2nd Avenue.
I drive to school.

I'm Adriano.
I'm from Italy.
I live in a house.
I live in New York on Broadway.
I take the bus to school.

C **Write and practice a conversation.**

Aki: Hi, Adriano. Where are you from?

Adriano: _____

Aki: _____

Adriano: _____

Aki: _____

Adriano: _____

D **Write.**

1. Aki _____ from Japan.

2. Adriano _____ from Italy.

3. Aki _____ in an apartment.

4. Aki _____ *drives* _____ to school.

5. Adriano _____ to school.

6. They _____ in New York.

Review

E **Read the map.**

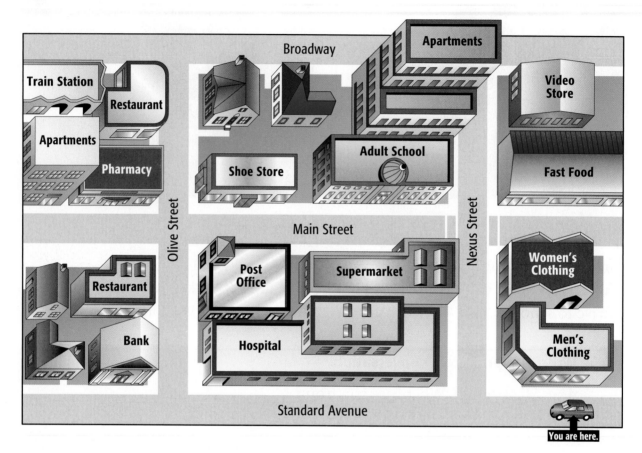

Broadway

Apartments

Train Station

Restaurant

Apartments

Pharmacy

Video Store

Fast Food

Shoe Store

Adult School

Olive Street

Nexus Street

Main Street

Restaurant

Post Office

Supermarket

Women's Clothing

Bank

Hospital

Men's Clothing

Standard Avenue

You are here.

F **Write the location.**

Location Name	Directions
post office	*Turn right on Nexus. Turn left on Main. It's next to the supermarket.*
1.	Go straight. Turn right on Olive Street. It's next to the restaurant.
2.	Go straight. Turn right on Olive Street. Turn right on Main Street. It's next to the adult school.
3.	Turn right on Nexus. Turn left on Broadway. It's next to the restaurant.

T E A M
P R O J E C T

Describing your community

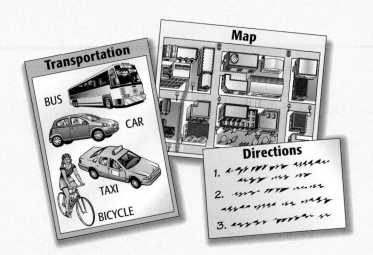

1. Form a team with four
   or five students.

   In your team, you need:

Position	Job	Student Name
Student 1 Leader	See that everyone speaks English. See that everyone participates.	
Student 2	Make a map.	
Student 3 Writer	Write directions.	
Student 4 Spokesperson	Prepare a presentation.	

2. Make a list of transportation in your community.

3. Make a map with the school in the middle. Write the names of stores
   and other places.

4. Write the directions from your school to three places in your community.

5. Present your project to the class.

PRONUNCIATION

Listen and repeat. Can you hear the syllables?

One Syllable	Two Syllables	Three Syllables
train	taxi	pharmacy
bank	city	apartment
house	hotel	bicycle

Listen. How many syllables do you hear? Circle *1, 2,* or *3.*

1. 1   2   3   **3.** 1   2   3

2. 1   2   3   **4.** 1   2   3

LEARNER LOG

Write the page number(s).

	Page Number(s)
1. stores and places to eat	_____
2. houses, apartments	_____
3. cars, trains, buses	_____
4. He walks to school.	_____
5. Where's the supermarket?	_____

My favorite lesson in this unit is _____ .

UNIT
6

Healthy Living

GOALS

- Identify body parts
- Identify common ailments
- Use the present continuous
- Talk about remedies
- Use the negative simple present

LESSON **I need a checkup.**

GOAL ▶ Identify body parts   *Vocabulary*

 A **Look at the picture.**

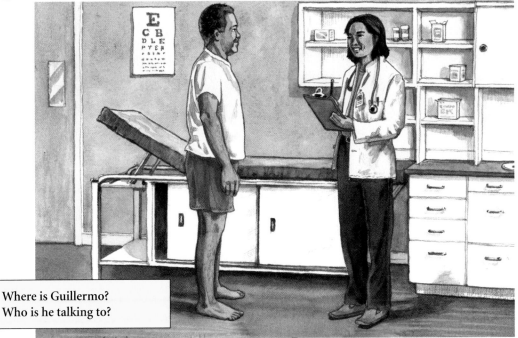

Where is Guillermo?
Who is he talking to?

  B **Listen and read.**

My name is Guillermo. I live in Chicago. I see the doctor once a year for a checkup. I'm very healthy.

C Read the new words. Listen and repeat.

head	back	hand	foot
neck	arm	leg	nose

D Write the new words in the picture.

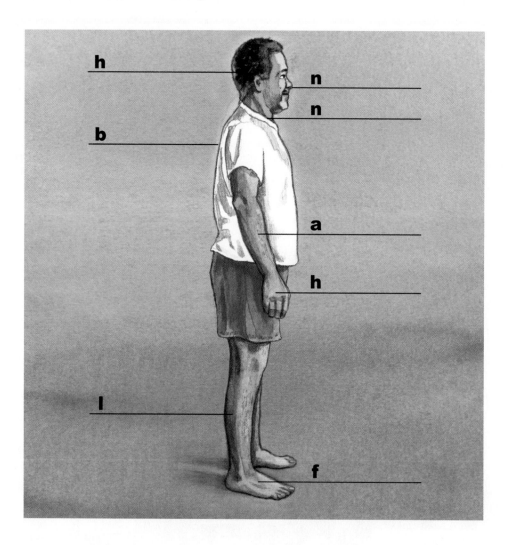

E   **Read.**

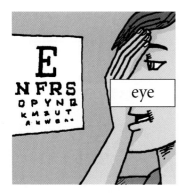
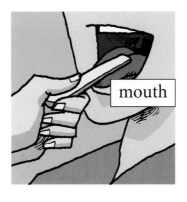
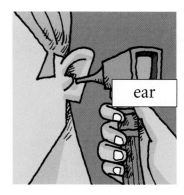

eye   mouth   ear

Please read the chart.   Please open your mouth and say *ah*.   Let me look in your ear.

 F   **Listen and practice the conversation.**

Doctor: Please sit down.
Guillermo: OK.
Doctor: <u>Please open your mouth and say *ah*</u>.
Guillermo: <u>Ah</u>.

G   **Practice the conversation with new words and actions.**

 H   **Write the name of the body part you hear.**

1. _____

2. _____

3. _____

4. _____

5. _____

6. _____

GOAL ▶ **Identify common ailments**   *Life Skill*

  A **Listen and repeat.**

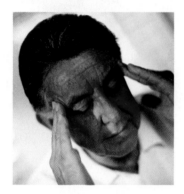

headache

backache

stomachache

cold (runny nose)

fever

  B **Listen and point.**

C **Read the conversation. Practice with new words.**

Maritza: How are you?
Shan: I'm sick!
Maritza: What's the matter?
Shan: I have a headache.

D **Read the charts.**

Simple Present (Regular)		
Subject	**Verb**	**Example sentence**
I, you, we, they	**see**	I see the doctor once a year.
	visit	We visit the doctor once a year.
he, she, it	**sees**	He sees the doctor once a week.
	visits	She visits the doctor once a week.

Simple Present (Irregular)		
Subject	***be* verb**	**Example sentence**
I	**am**	I am sick.
you, we, they	**are**	We are sick.
he, she, it	**is**	He is sick.

Simple Present (Irregular)		
Subject	***have* verb**	**Example sentence**
I, you, we, they	**have**	They have a headache.
he, she, it	**has**	She has a runny nose.

E **Write.**

1. He ___*has*___ (have) a headache.

2. She _____ (be) very sick.

3. We _____ (see) the doctor.

4. They _____ (have) problems.

5. I _____ (be) sick.

6. You _____ (have) a cold.

7. Oscar _____ (have) a stomachache.

8. Maritza _____ (visit) the doctor once a year.

9. You _____ (be) sick.

10. They _____ (want) a doctor.

11. We _____ (be) tired.

12. I _____ (like) my doctor.

13. The student _____ (have) a fever.

14. He _____ (be) a good doctor.

F Listen and bubble in the correct answer.

1. Maritza has
   - ○ a cold.
   - ○ a headache.
   - ○ a fever.

2. Shan has
   - ○ a backache.
   - ○ a fever.
   - ○ a cold.

3. John has
   - ○ a runny nose.
   - ○ a fever.
   - ○ a headache.

4. Anakiya has
   - ○ a fever.
   - ○ a runny nose.
   - ○ a backache.

G How many times a year are you sick? Write.

Headache	Stomachache	Backache	Fever	Cold

H Talk to four students.

A: What's your name?
B: John.
A: John, how often do you have a headache?
B: I have a headache four times a year.

once	a year
two times	a month
three times	a week
four times	a day

Name	Headache	Stomachache	Backache	Fever	Cold

 LESSON 3 # I have an appointment.

GOAL ▶ **Use the present continuous**

*Grammar*

A **Use the words in the box and talk about the picture.**

| talk | wait | read | answer | sleep |

 B **Listen to the conversation. What words do you hear first? Write 1–5.**

_____ talking

___*1*___ waiting

_____ reading

_____ answering

_____ sleeping

Read the chart.

Present Continuous (right now)			
Pronoun	***be* verb**	**Base + *ing***	**Example sentence**
I	am	talking	I am talking.
he, she, it,	is	sleeping	He is sleeping.
we, you, they	are	waiting	They are waiting.

D **Look at the picture on page 107. Write.**

1. The receptionist _is_ _answering_ (answer) the phone now.

2. The man in the white shirt ___ _____ (sleep) in the chair now.

3. The people ___ _____ (wait) for the doctor now.

4. The women ___ _____ (talk) about their children now.

5. Antonio ___ _____ (read) a magazine now.

E **Talk to a partner.**

What is the receptionist doing now?

What is the man in the white shirt doing now?

What are the people doing now?

What are the women doing now?

What is Antonio doing now?

Look at the picture.

G **Talk about the picture with a partner.**

H **Write what you and other students are doing in your classroom right now.**

_____

_____

_____

_____

_____

_____

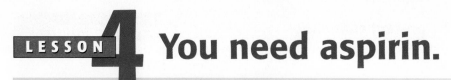

LESSON 4 You need aspirin.

A Read, listen, and write the missing words.

FEBRUARY 18

Name	Time	Problem	Phone
Julio Rodriguez	3:30	*	(777) 555-1395
Huong Pham	4:00	fever	(777) 555-3311
Richard Price	4:30	*	(777) 555-2323
Mele Ikahihifo	5:00	sore thoat and cough	(777) 555-5511
Fred Wharton	5:30	*	(777) 555-9764
Ayumi Tanaka	6:00	backache	(777) 555-8765

B Write.

_____fever_____   _____   _____

_____   _____   _____

C Write sentences.

1. _Julio has a headache._ _____

2. _Richard has_ _____

3. _Ayumi_ _____

D **Look at the medicine.**

Caution: Do not take more than four times a day.

E **Write other types of medicine you use.**

_____ _____ _____

F **In a group, write a good medicine for each illness.**

Illness	Medicine
headache	
fever	
stomachache	
sore throat and cough	
cold	

Read.

Simple Present		
Subject	**Verb**	**Example sentence**
I, you, we, they	need	I need aspirin.
he, she, it	need**s**	He needs antacid.

H **Write. Use** *need.*

1. Julio has a headache. *He needs aspirin.*

2. Huong has a fever. *He* _____.

3. Richard has a stomachache. *He* _____.

4. Mele has a sore throat and cough. *She* _____.

5. Fred has a cold. *He* _____.

6. Ayumi and Sue have backaches. *They* _____.

7. Tami and I have stomachaches. *We* _____.

8. Shiuli and Sang have sore throats. *They* _____.

I **Practice the conversation for all the appointments.**

Doctor: What's the matter?
Julio: I have a headache.
Doctor: You need aspirin.

J **Active Task:** What types of medicine do you have at home? Write.

_____ _____ _____

_____ _____ _____

GOAL ▷ Use the negative simple present   *Grammar*

 A   Read and listen.

HEALTH TIPS

We are happy you are a patient of Dr. Ramsey. Our goal is to help you stay healthy. Follow these suggestions and you will be healthier.

DOs

Sleep
Sleep 7-8 hours a day.

Exercise
Walk, run, or exercise 30 minutes a day.

Eat
Eat three good meals a day.

See the doctor
See the doctor once a year for a checkup.

DON'Ts

Don't smoke

For emergency appointments call 720-555-4311.

B **Listen and read Huong's story. Why is Huong healthy?**

    I'm healthy. I exercise one hour every day. I eat breakfast and dinner. I don't eat lunch. I don't smoke. I sleep seven hours every night.

C **What does Huong do? Fill in the chart.**

Yes	No
exercise	

D **Read the chart.**

Simple Present		
Subject	**Verb**	**Example sentence**
I, you, we, they	eat	I eat three meals every day.
he, she, it	sleep**s**	She sleeps seven hours every night.

Negative Simple Present		
Subject	**Verb**	**Example sentence**
I, you, we, they	**don't** eat	We don't eat three meals every day.
he, she, it	**doesn't** sleep**s̶**	He doesn't sleep seven hours every day.

E **Write about Huong.**

1. Huong ____exercises____ (exercise) one hour every day.

2. Huong _____ (sleep) seven hours every night.

3. Huong _____ (eat) breakfast and dinner.

4. Huong _____ (smoke).

5. Huong _____ (eat) lunch.

Read.

Name: Julia
Sleep: 8 hours
Meals: breakfast, lunch, dinner
Exercise: 30 minutes per day
Checkup: 1 time per year
Smoke: no

Name: Hasna
Sleep: 6 hours
Meals: lunch, dinner
Exercise: 0 minutes
Checkup: 1 time per year
Smoke: no

Name: Dalmar
Sleep: 8 hours
Meals: breakfast, lunch, dinner
Exercise: 20 minutes per day
Checkup: 0 times per year
Smoke: yes

G **Write.**

1. Julia and Hasna ___*don't smoke*___ (smoke).

2. Hasna _____ (eat) breakfast.

3. Dalmar and Julia _____ (sleep) eight hours every night.

4. Hasna _____ (exercise).

5. Julia and Hasna _____ (see) the doctor for a checkup.

6. Dalmar _____ (see) the doctor for a checkup.

H **Write.**

Your name: _____   Exercise: _____

Sleep: _____   Checkup: _____

Meals: _____   Smoke: _____

Review

A Write the body parts.

B Write the ailment.

EXAMPLE: stomach: _____ *stomachache* _____

head: _____

back: _____

throat: _____

nose: _____

C Complete the sentences with the present continuous.

1. The receptionist ___ _____ (talk) on the phone.

2. The patient ___ _____ (sleep).

3. The friends ___ _____ (wait) for the doctor.

4. Antonio and Erika ___ _____ (ask) about their children.

5. Hector ___ _____ (read) a magazine.

6. Sam and Julie ___ _____ (talk) to their mother.

D Write.

1. Richard has a headache. What does he need?

Medicine: _____

2. Orlando has a stomachache. What does he need?

Medicine: _____

3. Hue has a fever. What does she need?

Medicine: _____

4. Chan has a sore throat. What does he need?

Medicine: _____

E Read and write in the chart.

Jeremiah is not very healthy. He smokes a cigarette 10 times a day. He doesn't exercise. He eats three meals a day. He doesn't sleep 8 hours a night. He doesn't drink water. He sees the doctor once a year.

Yes	No

F **Complete the sentences with the simple present.**

1. She _____ (have) a headache.

2. They _____ (need) medicine.

3. We _____ (be) sick.

4. I _____ (be) healthy.

5. You _____ (exercise) every day.

6. Mario and Maria _____ (visit) the doctor once a year.

7. He _____ (sleep) eight hours a night.

8. Alfonso _____ (see) the doctor once a week.

G **Complete the sentences with the negative simple present.**

1. He _____ (smoke).

2. They _____ (eat) breakfast.

3. We _____ (need) medicine.

4. They _____ (exercise).

5. Nga _____ (have) a headache.

6. She _____ (visit) the doctor.

7. I _____ (want) lunch.

8. You _____ (exercise).

Name	Time	Problem	Phone
Julio Rodriguez	3:30	*	(777) 555-1395
Huong Pham	4:00	fever	(777) 555-3311
Richard Price	4:30	*	(777) 555-2323
Mele Ikahihifo	5:00	sore thoat and cough	(777) 555-5511
Fred Wharton	5:30	*	(777) 555-9764
Ayumi Tanaka	6:00	backache	...8765

FEBRUARY 18

Making appointments

1. Form a team with four or five students.

   In your team, you need:

Position	Job	Student Name
Student 1 Leader	See that everyone speaks English. See that everyone participates.	
Student 2 Artist	Make an appointment book page.	
Student 3 Writer	Write conversations to act out.	
Student 4 Spokesperson	Prepare a presentation.	

2. Prepare your roles.

   Who is the doctor? _____   Who is patient 2? _____

   Who is patient 1? _____   Who is the receptionist? _____

3. Make an appointment book page.

   What is patient 1's name?

   When is the appointment?

   What is the problem?

   Write a conversation between the receptionist and patient 1.

   Write another conversation between the doctor and patient 1.

4. Write conversations for patient 2.

5. Present your conversations and appointment book to the class.

PRONUNCIATION

Listen to the /g/ and /k/ sounds in these words. Can you hear the difference? Listen and repeat.

good   could   cold   gold   leg   lake   bag   back

Listen and circle the sound you hear.

1. /g/   /k/   **2.** /g/   /k/   **3.** /g/   /k/   **4.** /g/   /k/

LEARNER LOG

Write the page number(s).

	Page Number(s)
1. head, back, hand	_____
2. cold, fever	_____
3. is talking, is reading	_____
4. aspirin, antacid	_____
5. don't, doesn't	_____

My favorite lesson in this unit is _____.

G O A L S
- Identify occupations
- Ask information questions
- Identify job duties
- Use *can* and *can't*
- Use affirmative and negative commands

LESSON **1** Do you work?

GOAL ▶ Identify occupations

Vocabulary

 A Talk about the picture.

 B Listen and read.

My name is Emilio. I live in Dallas, Texas. I have a new job. I'm a cashier at Ultra Supermarket on Broadway!

 C What does Emilio do? Write.

1. He's a student.

2. He's a _____.

D Listen and repeat the words. What do these people do?

cashier   doctor   bus driver

student   salesperson   teacher

 E Who works here? Write the names of workers in the chart.

School (See Unit 2)	Restaurant (See Unit 3)	Clothing Store (See Unit 4)	Community (See Unit 5)	Health (See Unit 6)
teacher				

F   **Practice the vocabulary from Exercise D.**

Student A: What does <u>Emilio</u> do?
Student B: He's a <u>cashier</u>.

G   **Read the conversation.**

Student A: Do you work?
Student B: Yes, I'm a cashier. How about you? Do you work?
Student A: No, I'm a student.

H   **Practice the conversation with ten students.**

Name	Occupation

I   **Write sentences from Exercise H.**

EXAMPLE: Emilio is a cashier.

J   **Active Task:** What do your friends and family do for work? Make a list.

GOAL ▶ Ask information questions   *Grammar*

 A **Listen and repeat.**

receptionist

custodian

manager

nurse

 B **Listen and point to the picture.**

C **Read the conversation.**

Nurse: Excuse me. Can you help me?
Doctor: Sure.
Nurse: What do I write on this line?
Doctor: The patient's symptoms.
Nurse: Thanks for your help.

D **Listen and then practice the conversation.**

Employee: Excuse me. Can I ask you a question?
Manager: Sure.
Employee: When do I take my lunch break?
Manager: At 1 P.M.
Employee: OK, thanks.

 E **Read.**

Questions		
When	do I	take my lunch break?
Where	do I	find the mop? put the mail?
What	do I	write on this line?

F **Match the questions and answers.**

1. When do I take my lunch break?   the patient's symptoms

2. Where do I find the mop?   in the mail room

3. What do I write on this line?   at 1 P.M.

4. Where do I put the mail?   at 9:30 in the morning

5. When do I open the store?   the patient files

6. What do I put in this drawer?   in the closet

G **Practice new conversations. Use the questions and answers in Exercise F.**

A. Excuse me. Can I ask you a question?
B. Sure.
A. <u>When do I take my lunch break?</u>
B. <u>At 1 P.M.</u>
A. OK, thanks.

 Read.

My name is Amy. I'm a receptionist. I start work at 8:00. I work in an office and answer phones.

Answer the questions.

1. What does Amy do? _She's a_ _____.

2. When does she start work? _at_ _____

3. Where does she work? _in an_ _____

  Listen and answer the questions about Tan, Maria, and Alfredo.

	What	**When**	**Where**
Tan			
Maria			
Alfredo			

J **Answer the questions.**

1. When do you start work or school? _____

2. Where do you eat lunch? _____

3. When do you eat lunch? _____

4. Where do you take your lunch break? _____

5. When do you finish work? _____

What do they do?

GOAL ▶ **Identify job duties**

Life Skill

A Listen and point.

answers the phone

mops the floor

types letters

talks to customers

B What do they do? Write.

Occupation	Job Description
administrative assistant	*types letters*
receptionist	
custodian	
salesperson	

Read.

A receptionist files papers.

Sometimes workers take breaks.

 Read.

	mops	answers phones	talks to customers	types letters	takes breaks	files papers
salesperson			X		X	
administrative assistant		X		X	X	X
receptionist		X	X		X	X
custodian	X				X	

E **Answer the questions *Yes* or *No*.**

	Yes	No
1. Does the manager file?		X
2. Does the administrative assistant take breaks?		
3. Does the custodian talk to customers?		
4 Does the receptionist talk to customers?		
5. Does the administrative assistant mop the floor?		
6. Does the manager answer phones?		

F **Read the form.**

Work Evaluation

Name: *Emilio Sanchez*

Helps customers	(yes) no
Comes to work on time	(yes) no
Speaks English *well*	(yes) no
Follows directions *well*	(yes) no

Manager Signature: *Calvin Carter*

G **What does a good student do? Circle.**

files	practices English
(listens)	takes lunch breaks
cleans the office	follows directions
types letters	writes in class
does homework	reads in class
talks to customers	speaks in class
comes to school on time	answers phones

H **What do you do well?**

_____

_____

_____

LESSON 4 **I can't come to work.**

GOAL ▶ Use *can* and *can't*   **Grammar**

A Read.

> May 14
>
> Dear Mr. Mitchell,
>
>   I'm sorry I can't come to work tomorrow. I have a doctor's appointment. I can come to work on Wednesday.
>
>   Sincerely,
>   Emilio Sanchez

B Listen and write *1, 2,* or *3.*

_____ I have a doctor's appointment.

_____ My child's sick.

_____ I have a family emergency.

C Bubble in the correct answer.

1. Emilio can't come to work _____.
   ○ on Wednesday   ○ tomorrow   ○ today

2. Mr. Mitchell is _____.
   ○ a doctor   ○ a manager   ○ a custodian

3. Emilio can work _____.
   ○ on Wednesday   ○ tomorrow   ○ today

D **Read.**

Pronoun	*Can*	Verb (base)	Example Sentence
I, you, he, she, it, we, they	**can**	come	You can come.
		eat	They can eat.

Pronoun	*Can + not*	Verb (base)	Example Sentence
I, you, he, she, it, we, they	**can't**	come	We can't come.
		eat	She can't eat.

E **Complete the sentences with *can* + the verb.**

1. He _____*can come*_____ (come) to work on Wednesday.

2. They _____ (type) letters.

3. We _____ (eat) in the cafeteria.

4. I _____ (mop) the floor.

5. You _____ (follow) directions.

6. Maria and Chan _____ (speak) English.

F **Complete the sentences with *can't* + the verb.**

1. Emilo _____ (work) at 7:00.

2. Amy and Melissa _____ (type).

3. We _____ (talk) to customers.

4. They _____ (eat) after work.

5. I _____ (sleep) at work.

6. You _____ (wash) your hands.

G **Read what Emilio can do.**

My name is Emilio. I'm a cashier. I can count money. I can talk to customers in English. I can't type or file papers.

H **Answer the questions.**

What's the date today? _____

What's your manager's name (or your teacher's name)? _____

I **Write a letter to your manager or to your teacher like the one in Exercise A.**

Date: _____

Dear _____ ,

_____

_____

_____

_____

_____

Sincerely,

_____

Please type this letter.

GOAL ▶ **Use affirmative and negative commands** *Grammar*

 A Listen and point.

1. Don't smoke.

2. Wash your hands.

3. Don't file the papers.

4. Fred, please answer the phones.

5. Fred, please type these letters.

6. Don't eat in the office.

 B Read the signs and notes. Circle *Yes* or *No*.

1. Don't smoke.	Yes	(No)
2. Wash hands.	Yes	No
3. Don't file.	Yes	No
4. Answer the phones.	Yes	No
5. Type letters.	Yes	No
6. Don't eat.	Yes	No

C Read.

Affirmative Commands			
	Verb		**Example sentence**
~~You~~	Wash	your hands.	Wash your hands.
	Answer	the phones.	Answer the phones.
	Type	the letters.	Type the letters.

Negative Commands				
		Verb		**Example sentence**
~~You~~	Don't	wash	your hands.	Don't wash your hands.
		answer	the phones.	Don't answer the phones.
		type	the letters.	Don't type the letters.

D Read the job description.

RECEPTIONIST JOB DESCRIPTION
WINTER HOLIDAY HOTEL
2900 W. EDEN BLVD.
SACRAMENTO, CA 94203

Position: #33

Job Title: Receptionist

Hours: 9:00 A.M. – 6:00 P.M.

1. Answer phones.
2. Use office machines (fax/copier).
3. Talk to customers.
4. File.
5. Come to work on time. Don't come to work late!
6. Take one 60-minute lunch break. Don't eat in the office.
7. Take two 15-minute breaks. Don't take one 30-minute break.
8. Don't smoke in the office.

E **Look at the job description (in Exercise D). Write the commands.**

Do's	Don'ts
Answer phones	

F **Read the conversation.**

Manager: How are you, Fred?
Receptionist: I'm fine, thank you.
Manager: Please, <u>answer the phones today</u>.
Receptionist: Yes, of course.

G **Practice the conversation with information from Exercise A on page 133.**

H **In groups write classroom do's and don'ts.**

Classroom Do's	Classroom Don'ts
Listen	

Review

A Write the name of the job.

1.
_____

2.
_____

3.
_____

4.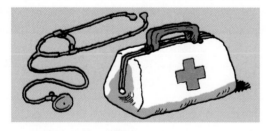
_____

5.
_____

6.
_____

7.
_____

8.
_____

B Ask a partner to point to a picture.

Student A: What does he do?
Student B: He's a custodian.

Review

C   Match the job with the duty. Draw a line.

1.

a. types letters

2.

b. counts money

3.

c. mops the floor

4.

d. talks to customers

D   Write *When* or *Where*.

1. _____ does the store open? The store opens at 10:00 A.M.

2. _____ do you take a break? I take a break in the cafeteria.

3. _____ do you work? I work in Sacramento.

4. _____ does he sit? He sits over there.

5. _____ does she type letters? She types letters in the afternoon.

Review

E Write four things your partner can do.

_____

_____

_____

_____

F Write one thing your partner can't do.

_____

G Write.

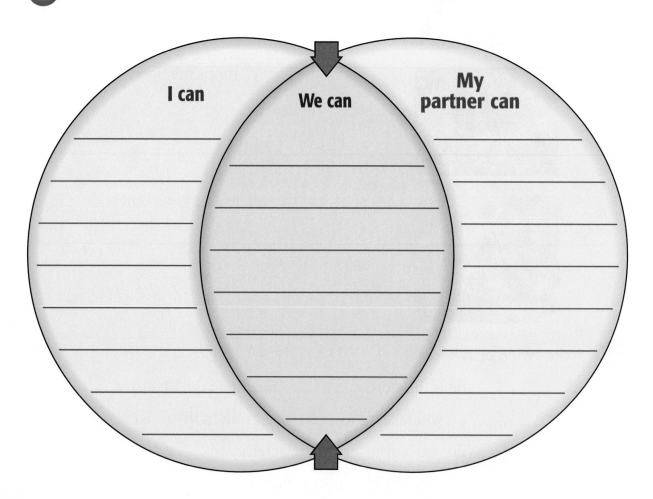

I can

We can

My partner can

T E A M
P R O J E C T

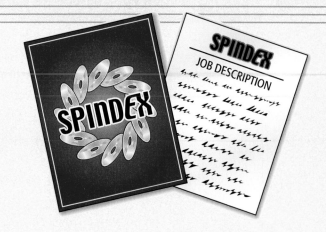

Starting a company

1. Form a team with four or five students.

   In your team, you need:

Position	Job	Student Name
Student 1 Leader	See that everyone speaks English. See that everyone participates.	
Student 2 Artist	Make a title page with the name of your company and a logo.	
Student 3 Writer	Write job descriptions.	
Student 4 Spokesperson	Prepare a presentation.	

2. What is the name of your company? _____
   What is your company logo? Make a title page.

3. What are your occupations in the company?

4. Write three job descriptions for your jobs.

5. Present your company to the class.

PRONUNCIATION

Listen for *can* and *can't* in these sentences. Can you hear the difference?

Emily **can** come on Wednesday.   George **can** speak English well.
Emily **can't** come on Sunday.   George **can't** speak Spanish well.

Listen and write *can* or *can't*.

1. We _____ eat in class.

2. Tina _____ understand French.

3. I _____ meet you after work.

4. I _____ type very well.

LEARNER LOG

Write the page number(s).

	Page Number(s)
1. occupations	_____
2. when, where	_____
3. mop, file, talk, type	_____
4. can, can't	_____
5. Do's and Don'ts	_____

My favorite lesson in this unit is _____.

Lifelong Learning and Review

GOALS

- Organize study materials
- Review: Make purchases
- Review: Give and follow directions
- Make goals
- Develop a study schedule

LESSON 1 · Let's get organized!

GOAL ▶ Organize study materials   *Life Skill*

A Listen and repeat.

binder

dividers

sheet of lined paper

B Write three items you use to organize your study materials.

_____

_____

_____

C **Listen and bubble in.**

1. What size binder do they need?
   ○ 1 inch
   ○ 1½ inches
   ○ 3 inches

2. How many dividers do they need?
   ○ 1 divider
   ○ 3 dividers
   ○ 5 dividers

3. How many sheets of lined paper
   do they need?
   ○ 50 sheets
   ○ 100 sheets
   ○ 200 sheets

D **Make a binder with the section titles below. Write the page numbers and two words for each section in your binder.**

Section	Pages in this book	Example Vocabulary
Personal Information	1–40	_____ _____
Consumer Economics (FOOD/CLOTHING)		_____ _____
Community Resources		_____ _____
Health		_____ _____
Occupational Knowledge		_____ _____

Interview and write about your partner.

1. What's your name? _____

2. Where do you live? _____

3. What is your phone number? _____

4. What is your birth date? _____

5. Are you married? _____

6. Where are you from? _____

 Make the first page in your binder on another sheet of paper for Personal Information.

PERSONAL PROFILE

_____
SCHOOL

PHOTO

_____
TEACHER

NAME _____
       First   Middle   Last

ADDRESS _____

CITY _____ STATE _____ ZIP _____

COUNTRY *I'm from* _____

MARITAL STATUS *(Circle)*   Single   Married   Divorced

LESSON 2 I need paper.

GOAL ▶ Make purchases

Life Skill

A Read the ads.

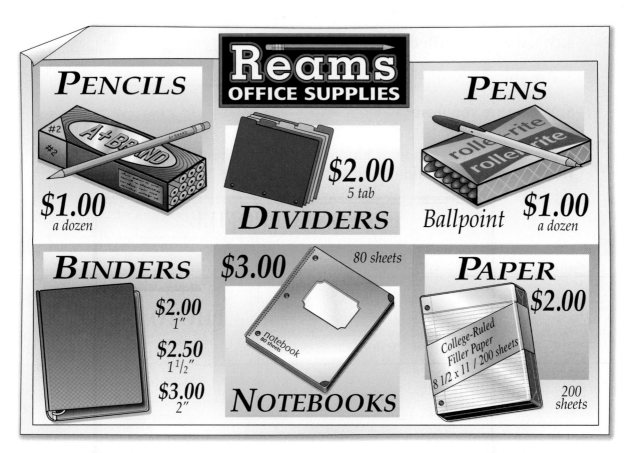

How much **is** the paper?	How much **are** the notebooks?

 B Listen to the conversation and practice.

Customer: Excuse me, how much are the dividers?

Salesperson: They are $2.00 for a set of five.

Customer: Thanks. I need one set please.

> a 2" binder = a two-inch binder

C **Listen and repeat.**

I need . . .

. . . a box of pencils.

. . . a 2-inch binder.

. . . a set of five colored dividers.

. . . a package of paper.

. . . a box of ballpoint pens.

. . . a notebook.

D **What do you need? Write.**

Reams OFFICE SUPPLIES

Item	Quantity	Price
2" binder	1	$3.00
TOTAL		

CUSTOMER COPY

E **Practice the conversation. Use information from Exercise A on page 144.**

Salesperson: What do you need?

Customer: I need a <u>2-inch binder.</u>

Salesperson: They are over here.

Customer: How much are they?

Salesperson: They are <u>$3.00</u> each.

F **Active Task:** Go to the store and buy office supplies.

G   In a group, make a list of food you buy in the supermarket.

Food	Price

H   In a group, make a list of clothing you buy in a clothing store.

Clothing	Price

I   Write and practice new conversations at the store with food and clothing.

J   Prepare a section in your binder for Consumer Economics.

Consumer Economics

Stand Out Basic Page Numbers

Important Vocabulary

Food:
apples

Clothing:
shoes

Sentences and Questions

What's for lunch?
I need a blue shirt.

Consumer Economics

Grammar
Preposition of location   Page Number: _____

Singular and Plural   Page Number: _____

Simple Present — like   Page Number: _____

LESSON **3** Where's the office supply store?

GOAL ▶ **Give and follow directions**

Life Skill

A Look at the picture.

 B Listen to the conversation. Write.

Paul: Excuse me, where is Reams Office Supplies?

Linda: It's on First Street.

Paul: On First Street?

Linda: Yes, go straight on this street. Turn _____ on Main Street
and _____ on First. It's _____ the video store.

Paul: Thanks.

Read.

CITY PHONE DIRECTORY

Nursing Schools		Optometrists	

Ace Nursing Schools
8237 Beachnut Ave. 555-6732

Metropolitan Nursing
2467 Apple Lane 555-3472

Office Supplies

Pencil Head Stationers
11 Broadway 555-3411

Nottingham Paper
23400 Portland Ave. 555-0045

Reams Office Supplies
1717 First St. 555-2762

Dr. Michael's Eye Exams
1723 First St. 555-3310

Quick Check Glasses
3456 W. Circle Ave. 555-6776

Painting Supplies

Bill's Painting Supply
5678 First St. 555-1301

Paint for Less
15 Broadway 555-3737

Picture Perf~
~63.7~

D **Read the conversation.**

Paul: Excuse me, where is <u>Reams Office Supplies</u>?
Linda: It's on <u>First Street</u>.
Paul: What's the address?
Linda: It's <u>1717 First Street</u>.
Paul: Thanks.

E **Practice new conversations with the information in Exercise C.**

F   Draw a map from your school to an office supply store in your community.

G   Write directions to an office supply store.

_____

_____

_____

_____

H   Prepare a section in your binder for Community Resources.

Community

Stand Out Basic Page Numbers _____

Important Vocabulary

left

_____ _____ _____ _____
_____ _____ _____ _____
_____ _____ _____ _____
_____ _____ _____ _____
_____ _____ _____ _____
_____ _____ _____ _____

Sentences and Questions

What's for lunch?
I need a blue shirt. _____ _____
_____ _____
_____ _____
_____ _____
_____ _____

Community

Grammar
in/on   Page Number: _____

Simple Present   Page Number: _____

_____   Page Number: _____

Sleep eight hours a day.

GOAL ▶ **Make goals**

A **Read Liang's goals.**

My Goals

- ☑ Sleep eight hours a day.
- ☐ Go to school every day.
- ☐ Exercise one hour a day.
- ☑ Eat three good meals a day.
- ☐ Study English at home one hour a day.
- ☑ Read the newspaper in English 15 minutes a day.
- ☐ Watch TV 15 minutes a day.

 B **Listen to Carina and check three goals.**

☐ Sleep eight hours a day.

☐ Go to school every day.

☐ Exercise one hour a day.

☐ Eat three good meals a day.

☐ Study English at home one hour a day.

☐ Read the newspaper in English 15 minutes a day.

☐ Watch TV 15 minutes a day.

C **Talk about Liang's and Carina's goals.**

EXAMPLE: Liang's goal is to sleep eight hours a day.

D Read about Liang's class. Talk about the bar graphs.

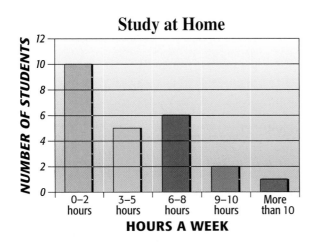

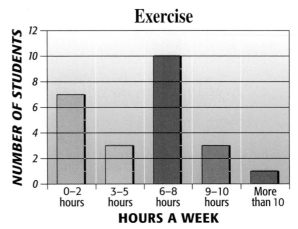

E Take a class poll. Make a bar graph.

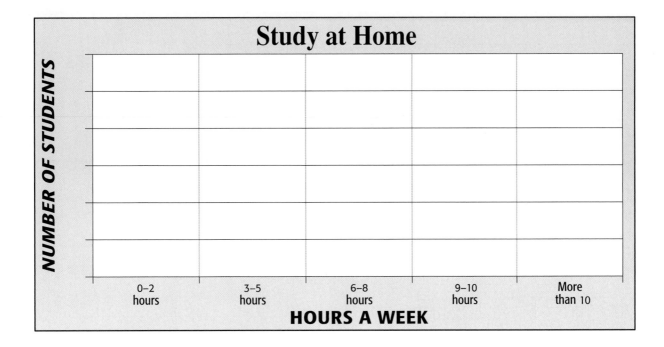

F   **Interview a partner.**

How many hours do you exercise every day? _____

How many hours do you sleep every day? _____

How many hours do you study every day? _____

How many meals do you eat every day? _____

How many days do you go to school a week? _____

G   **Write your goals.**

_____

_____

_____

_____

_____

_____

H   **Prepare a section in your binder for Health.**

Health

Stand Out Basic Page Numbers _____

Important Vocabulary

Sentences and Questions

Health

Grammar
Simple Present   Page Number: _____

Negative Simple Present   Page Number: _____

Present Continuous   Page Number: _____

LESSON 5 When can I study?

GOAL ▶ Develop a study schedule

Life Skill

A Listen and point to the vocabulary.

Teacher and Student Duties

help students	study at home	come to class on time
learn new words	prepare lessons	do homework

B Write.

Student Duties	Teacher Duties
	help students

C Add more duties to the list in Exercise B.

Read and talk about the schedule. When does Liang work? When does Liang go to school?

LIANG'S SCHEDULE

	Sunday	Monday	Tuesday	Wednesday	Thursday	Friday	Saturday
6:00 A.M.	Breakfast	Breakfast	Breakfast	Breakfast	Breakfast	Breakfast	Breakfast
9:00 A.M.		School	School	School	School	Study	Study
11:00 A.M.	Lunch	Lunch	Lunch	Lunch	Lunch	Lunch	Lunch
1:00 P.M.		Study	Study	Study	Study	Study	Study
3:00 P.M.							
5:00 P.M.		Work	Work	Work	Work	Work	
7:00 P.M.	Dinner	Dinner	Dinner	Dinner	Dinner	Dinner	Dinner
9:00 P.M.							

E **Answer the questions.**

1. When do you study at school? _____

2. When do you study at home? _____

3. When do you work? _____

4. When do you eat breakfast, lunch, and dinner? _____

F **Complete your schedule.**

MY SCHEDULE

	Sunday	Monday	Tuesday	Wednesday	Thursday	Friday	Saturday

Read and talk about Liang's evaluation.

Name: _Liang Ochoa_

Studies at home	(Yes)	No
Comes to class on time	Yes	(No)
Speaks English in class	Yes	(No)
Is organized	(Yes)	No

Teacher's Signature: _Jennifer Douglas_

H **Ask questions about Liang.**

EXAMPLE: Does Liang study at home? Does Liang speak English in class?

I **Complete an evaluation about you. Ask your teacher to sign it.**

Name: _____

Studies at home	Yes	No
Comes to class on time	Yes	No
Speaks English in class	Yes	No
Is organized	Yes	No

Teacher's Signature: _____

J **Prepare a section in your binder for Occupational Knowledge.**

Occupational (Work) Knowledge

Stand Out Basic Page Numbers _____

Important Vocabulary

_____ _____ _____ _____
_____ _____ _____ _____
_____ _____ _____ _____
_____ _____ _____ _____

_____ _____ _____ _____
_____ _____ _____ _____
_____ _____ _____ _____

Sentences and Questions

_____ _____
_____ _____
_____ _____
_____ _____
_____ _____

Occupational (Work) Knowledge

Grammar
when/where   Page Number: _____

can/can't   Page Number: _____

Affirmative and negative instructions   Page Number: _____

Review

A **Match the meaning to the word. Draw a line.**

1. January, _____, March
2. This person answers phones in an office.
3. It is at the end of your arm.
4. Your home.
5. Milk, cheese, eggs
6. Not sunny
7. Medicine for a headache
8. A place for money
9. Food for a sandwich
10. Ten cents
11. This person works in a hospital.
12. May, _____, July
13. Clothing for winter
14. A place to buy food
15. You wear them on your feet.
16. You _____ a bicycle.

a. dairy
b. address
c. aspirin
d. bank
e. bread
f. dime
g. doctor
h. February
i. hand
j. June
k. rainy
l. receptionist
m. ride
n. shoes
o. supermarket
p. sweater

B **Practice with a partner.**

Student A: It is at the end of your arm.
Student B: hand

C **Find the page number for the words. (Look at the Vocabulary List on pages 162–163.)**

Word	Page Number	Word	Page Number
divorced		broccoli	
application		cash register	
foggy		healthy	
raise your hand		mop	

D Find the page number from the Vocabulary List on pages 162–163 and write the sentence.

Word: phone number

Page number: _14_

Sentence: _What's your phone number?_

Word: check

Page number: _73_

Sentence: _____

Word: go straight

Page number: ____

Sentence: _____

Word: checkup

Page number: ____

Sentence: _____

E Find two new words from the Vocabulary List on pages 162–163.

Word: _____

Page number: ____

Sentence: _____

Word: _____

Page number: ____

Sentence: _____

Review

F **Use the Grammar Reference on page 161 to fill in the blanks.**

1. a. I _____ married.

   b. We _____ students.

   c. You _____ hungry.

   d. They _____ thirsty.

   e. She _____ single.

2. a. I _____ milk.

   b. We _____ a bowl of soup.

   c. You _____ vegetables.

   d. They _____ tacos.

   e. She _____ a sandwich.

3. a. _____ your hands.

   b. _____ the phones.

   c. _____ letters.

4. a. I can _____.

   b. They can _____.

   c. We can't _____.

   d. She can't _____.

G **Write the plural forms.**

Singular	Plural
pear	
cookie	
banana	
egg	
tomato	

T E A M
P R O J E C T

Creating a study guide

1. Form a team with four or five students.

   In your team, you need:

Position	Job	Student Name
Student 1 Leader	See that everyone speaks English. See that everyone participates.	
Student 2 Writer	Organize and add sections of the study guide.	
Student 3 Artist	Decorate the study guide.	
Student 4 Spokesperson	Prepare a presentation.	

2. Complete your binder from this unit. Share the information from your binder with your group.

3. Use your binders to make a team binder. This will be a study guide for new students.

4. Decorate the study guide.

5. Present your study guide to the class.

PRONUNCIATION

Listen to the /sh/ and /ch/ sounds in these words. Can you hear the difference? Listen and repeat.

shoes choose   ships chips   wash watch   cash catch

Listen and circle /ch/ or /sh/.

1. /ch/   /sh/   **3.** /ch/   /sh/
2. /ch/   /sh/   **4.** /ch/   /sh/

LEARNER LOG

Write the page number(s).

	Page Number(s)
1. personal information	_____
2. How much is the binder?	_____
3. Where is the store?	_____
4. goals	_____
5. schedules	_____

My favorite lesson in this unit is _____.

Grammar Reference

The Simple Present—*be*

Subject	Verb	Contraction	Example sentence
I	**am**	I'm	I am (I'm) married.
he	**is**	he's	He is (He's) divorced.
she		she's	She is (She's) single.
we	**are**	we're	We are (We're) students.
you		you're	You are (You're) hungry.
they		they're	They are (They're) thirsty.

The Simple Present—*be* (negative)

Subject	Verb	Negative	Example sentence
I	**am**		I am (I'm) not married.
he	**is**		He is (He's) not divorced.
she		not	She is (She's) not single.
we			We are (We're) not students.
you	**are**		You are (You're) not hungry.
they			They are (They're) not thirsty.

Singular/Plural Nouns

Singular (one)	Plural (more than one)	*There is*	*There are*
egg	egg**s**	There **is** one blue dress.	There **are** two green shirts.
orange	orange**s**		
Exceptions			
potato/tomato	potato**es**/tomato**es**		
sandwich	sandwich**es**		

The Simple Present

Subject	Verb	Object	Example sentence
I, you, we, they	want/like/need	milk	I want milk.
he, she, it	want**s**/need**s**/like**s**	a sandwich	He needs a sandwich.

The Present Continuous (right now)

Subject	Verb	Base + *ing*	Example sentence
I	am	talking	I am talking.
he, she, it,	is	sleeping	He is sleeping.
we, you, they	are	waiting	They are waiting.

Commands (affirmative and negative)

	Verb		Example sentence
(You)	wash	your hands	Wash your hands.
(You)	don't wash	your hands	Don't wash your hands.

Modal Verbs (affirmative and negative)

Pronoun	*Can*	Verb (base)	Example sentence
I, you, he, she, it, we, they	can	come	I can come.
I, you, he, she, it, we, they	can't	sleep	They can't sleep.

Stand Out Basic Vocabulary List

Pre-Unit
Greetings
bye P2
goodbye P2
hello P2
hi P2
Study verbs
bubble in P6
circle P5
listen P3
point P6
practice P6
read P6
repeat P3
write P3

Unit 1
Calendar
date 4
day 6
month 4
week 6
year 4
Days
Sunday 4
Monday 4
Tuesday 4
Wednesday 4
Thursday 4
Friday 4
Saturday 4
Months
January 4
February 4
March 4
April 4
May 4
June 4
July 4
August 4
September 4
October 4
November 4
December 4
Marital status
divorced 7
married 7
single 7
Personal information
address 10
application 13
birth date 14
city 10

email address 16
name 1
phone number 14
state 10
zip code 10

Unit 2
country 21
from 21
live 23
Weather
cloudy 24
cold 24
foggy 24
hot 24
rainfall 26
rainy 24
snowy 25
sunny 25
windy 24
Classroom words
book 28
bookcase 34
computer 33
desk 33
file cabinet 34
listen 27
raise your hand 28
read 27
sit down 28
stand up 28
table 33
talk 27
trash can 34
write 27
Location
between 34
in 34
in the back 34
in the front 34
next to 34
on 34

Unit 3
hungry 44
thirsty 45
Food
apple 42
banana 46
bread 42
broccoli 50
butter 42
cake 53

candy 53
carrot 46
cheese 42
chicken 42
chips 44
chocolate 53
cookie 46
egg 42
fish 50
fries 44
fruit 44
ground beef 47
hamburger 44
ice cream 53
lettuce 42
mayonnaise 42
milk 42
onion 47
orange 42
pear 48
pepper 47
pie 53
potato 42
rice 44
salt 47
sandwich 41
spaghetti 47
strawberry 50
sundae 53
taco 44
tomato 47
turkey 41
vegetables 44
water 42
Meals
breakfast 43
dinner 43
lunch 43
Containers and measurements
jar 47
package 47
pound 47
Supermarket
dairy 50
meat 50

Unit 4
Clothing
blouse 62
coat 62
dress 62
pants 62

shirt 62
shoes 62
shorts 62
socks 62
sweater 62
Colors
black 65
blue 64
green 65
red 64
white 64
yellow 65
Shopping
cash register 67
check 73
receipt 69
sale 63
size 65
Money
dime 67
dollar 67
nickel 67
penny 67
quarter 67

Unit 5
Places in the community
bank 93
bookstore 93
bus stop 82
clothing store 81
fast food 82
hospital 93
hotel 82
pharmacy 81
post office 93
restaurant 82
shoe store 81
supermarket 81
telephone 82
video store 81
Housing
apartment 84
condominium 85
house 84
Transportation
drive a car 89
ride a bicycle 89
take a bus 89
take a taxi 89
take a train 89
walk 89

Stand Out Basic Listening Scripts

Pre-Unit
CD 1 Track 2, Page P2, Lesson 1, Exercise B
Mrs. Adams: Hello, I'm Mrs. Adams.
Orlando: Hi, Mrs. Adams, I'm Orlando. Nice to meet you.
Mrs. Adams: Nice to meet you, too.
Orlando: Bye.
Mrs. Adams: Goodbye.

CD 1 Track 4, Page P3, Lesson 2, Exercise B
1. A: Hello, I'm Mrs. Willis.
    B: Hello, Mrs. Willis, I'm Amal—A-M-A-L.
CD 1 Track 5
2. A: Hello, I'm Mrs. Adams.
    B: Hi, Mrs. Adams, I'm Orlando—
    O-R-L-A-N-D-O.
CD 1 Track 6
3. A: Hi, I'm Ms. Angela Ramos.
    B: Hello, Ms. Ramos, I'm Chinh—C-H-I-N-H.
CD 1 Track 7
4. Mr. Brown: Hi, I'm Mr. Brown.
    Elsa: Hi, Mr. Brown. I'm Elsa—E-L-S-A.
CD 1 Track 8
5. Jill: Hi, I'm Jill.
    Mrs. Adams: Hello, Jill. I'm Mrs. Adams—
    A-D-A-M-S.
CD 1 Track 9
6. Mr. Perez: Hello, I'm Mr. Perez.
    Fawzia: Hello, Mr. Perez. I'm Fawzia—F-A-W-Z-I-A.

CD 1 Track 11, Page P5, Lesson 3, Exercise B
Example: Giulia Sclippa is a new student at Locke Adult School. Her phone number is (714) 555-0971.
1. Andrew Keefer is a new student at West Palm Adult School. His phone number is (352) 555-6767.
2. Lisa Karamardian is a new student at Aloha Adult School. Her phone number is (808) 555-6755.

3. Bjorn Schlager is a new student at Arroyo Adult School. His phone number is (915) 555-3455.

CD 1 Track 12, Page P6, Lesson 4, Exercise B
Example 1: Please take out a piece of paper and write your name.
Example 2: Today we will practice saying names and addresses.
1. Please open your books and read Exercise 1.
2. When I say the word, I want you to point to the picture.

Unit 1
CD 1 Track 18, page 4, Lesson 2, Exercise D
March-December-February-November-September-June-January-July-May-April-August-October

CD 1 Track 19, page 6, Lesson 2, Exercise I
Amal: What's the date today?
Chinh: It's September 4, 2004.
Amal: Thanks.

CD 1 Track 21, Page 7, Lesson 3, Exercise A
Amal is a student at Locke Adult School. He is single. His birth date is August 3, 1982. He is from Saudi Arabia. Chinh is from Vietnam. Chinh and Jeff are married. They got married two years ago.
Mirna is from Russia. She is a student and wants to speak English better. She is divorced. She has three children.

CD 1 Track 22, Page 8, Lesson 3, Exercise C
1. Hans: Maria, are you single?
    Maria: No, I'm married.
CD 1 Track 23
2. Maria: Hans, are you married?
    Hans: No, I'm single.

CD 1 Track 24

3. Hans: Maria, is Ms. Taylor married?
   Maria: Yes, I think so.

CD 1 Track 25, Page 11, Lesson 4, Exercise D

Amal is a student at Locke Adult School. His address is 8237 Augustin Sreet, Irvine, California 92714.
Elsa is from Russia. She is a good student. Her address is 23 San Andrew Street, Irvine, California 92618.
Chinh is also a student at Locke Adult School. She lives at 23905 Fin Road, Irvine, California 92603.
Orlando is from Mexico. He is learning English. His address is 3321 Walker Avenue, Irvine, California, 92714.

CD 1 Track 29, Page 20, Pronunciation

1. I'm a student.   2. She is from Russia.   3. You're from India.   4. What's the date today?

Unit 2

CD 1 Track 30, Page 21, Lesson 1, Exercise A

Mr. Jackson: Hello, I'm Mr. Jackson. What's your name?
Concepcion: My name is Concepcion. I'm new in the class.
Mr. Jackson: Nice to meet you.
Concepcion: Thank you.
Mr. Jackson: Where are you from, Concepcion?
Concepcion: I'm from Cuba.
Mr. Jackson: That's great! Welcome to the class.

CD 1 Track 31, Page 22, Lesson 1, Exercise C

1. Mr Jackson: Hello, I'm Mr. Jackson. What's your name?
   Concepcion: My name is Concepcion. I'm new in the class.
   Mr. Jackson: Nice to meet you.
   Concepcion: Thank you.
   Mr. Jackson: Where are you from, Concepcion?
   Narrator: She is from Cuba. What's her name?

CD 1 Track 32

2. Mr. Jackson: Are you the new student from Canada?
   Julie: Yes, my name is Julie.
   Mr. Jackson: I hope you enjoy our class.
   Julie: I will. Thank you.
   Narrator: She is from Canada. What's her name?

CD 1 Track 33

3. Mr. Jackson: Hello, welcome to the class. What's your name?
   Shiro: I'm Shiro. I came to the United States last week.
   Mr. Jackson: Where are you from, Shiro?
   Shiro: I'm from Japan.
   Narrator: He is from Japan. What's his name?

CD 1 Track 34

4. Mr. Jackson: Hello, Edgar.
   Edgar: Hi, Mr. Jackson.
   Mr. Jackson: Edgar, where are you from?
   Edgar: I'm from Senegal.
   Narrator: He is from Senegal. What's his name?

CD 1 Track 35

5. Mr: Jackson: Hello, class. Please sit down and we will get started.
   Edgar: Excuse me, where are you from?
   Mr. Jackson: I'm from right here in Fort Lauderdale, Florida.
   Narrator: He is from Fort Lauderdale, Florida. What is his name?

CD 1 Track 38, Page 24, Lesson 2, Exercise B

This is Express Weather from Miami, Florida. We are happy to bring you the latest on weather throughout the world. Let's start with Havana, Cuba. It's hot and sunny today in Havana with a temperature of 98 degrees. In Tokyo, Japan, it is cloudy and unusually cold for this time of year. In Patagonia, Chile, be careful when traveling. It is very windy today. Moving along to the north of us in Montreal, Canada, the bitter cold is keeping everyone indoors. Yes, it's very cold. In Lisbon, Portugal, it's foggy at the waterfront, be careful when driving. In Mombasa, Kenya, it's rainy and the rain will continue for several days.

CD 1 Track 39, Page 25, Lesson 2, Exercise E

1. A: How's the weather?
   B: It's hot today.

CD 1 Track 40

2. A: How are you?
   B: I'm fine.
   A: How's the weather where you are?
   B: It's windy today.

CD 1 Track 41

3. A: Wow, what a storm yesterday.
   B: Yes, but today is much better.
   A: How's the weather outside?
   B: It's rainy today, but there is no storm.

CD 1 Track 42

4. A: It's a great day.
   B: I don't think so.
   A: Why not?
   B: It's cold today.

CD 1 Track 43, Page 27, Lesson 3, Exercise A

All the students work hard in Mr. Jackson's English class. Two students are talking in the back of the room about their homework. One student is writing at his desk. Shiro is at his desk, too. He is listening to a tape. Julie is reading. She is a good student.

CD 1 Track 44, Page 30, Lesson 4, Exercise A

Shiro has a busy schedule. He has English class at 9 A.M. At 12:00 he eats lunch. He goes to class again at 1:00 in the afternoon. He has pronunciation class. He goes to work at 4 P.M.

CD 1 Track 45, Page 32, Lesson 4, Exercise F
Cameron: Hi Julie, how are you?
Julie: Fine, thanks.
Cameron: What is your schedule today?
Julie: I have English class at 9:00, work at 11:00, lunch at 1:30, and finally I go to bed at 10:30 tonight.
Cameron: I see you are very busy. Maybe we could have lunch together at 1:30.
Julie: That would be great!

CD 1 Track 48, Page 33, Lesson 5, Exercise C
Mr. Jackson's English class is always very busy. There are two students in front of the board. Mr. Jackson is next to the door. There is a plant on his desk. The trash can is between the teacher's desk and the bookcase. The books are in the bookcase. There are three tables. Two chairs are next to one of the tables. There are computers on the other side of the room. There are two file cabinets in back of the computers.

Unit 3
CD 1 Track 54, Page 46, Lesson 2, Exercise G
1. Woman: I'm hungry.
   Man: Me, too. I really need something healthy.
   Woman: Carrots are healthy and they taste good!
CD 1 Track 55
2. Woman 1: I'm thirsty.
   Woman 2: Can I get you anything?
   Woman 1: Maybe some water?
   Woman 2: I'll get it right away.
CD 1 Track 56
3. Man 1: Do you have anything to eat?
   Man 2: Sure, but what do you want?
   Man 1: I don't know. I'm very hungry.
   Man 2: How about an apple?
   Man 1: Thanks.
CD 1 Track 57
4. Woman: My sister is very hungry. She needs to eat.
   Man: I have some bananas here. Would a banana be ok?
   Woman: That sounds great! Thanks!
   Man: I'll get her one.

CD 1 Track 59, Page 50, Lesson 4, Exercise A
In the fruit section, you will find: apples, oranges, strawberries, pears, and bananas. In the vegetable section, you will find: lettuce, carrots, broccoli, tomatoes, and potatoes. In the meat and fish section, you will find: ground beef, chicken, turkey, and fish. In the dairy section, you will find: cheese, milk, and yogurt.

CD 1 Track 60, Page 51, Lesson 4, Exercise F
Amadeo: Yoshi, I'm going to the supermarket. What do you want?
Yoshi: Um, I want some oranges, apples, and strawberries.
Amadeo: Is that all?

Yoshi: No. I think I want some yogurt, cheese, and eggs, too.
Amadeo: OK, is that it?
Yoshi: No. Get me some potatoes, fish, and water.
Amadeo: Anything else.
Yoshi: No, that's it.
Amadeo: Ok, let me read it back to you. You want oranges, apples, strawberries, yogurt, cheese, eggs, potatoes, fish, and water.
Yoshi: Yep, that's all!

CD 1 Track 62, Page 53, Lesson 5, Exercise B
Maria likes dessert. She especially likes cake.
She also likes sundaes.
She eats dessert after every meal.

CD 1 Track 63, Page 53, Lesson 5, Exercise C
1. Man: What dessert would you like?
   Woman: Well, I really like chocolate, but the apple pie looks good, too.
CD 1 Track 64
2. Woman: Just wait until you see what's for dessert.
   Man: What is it?
   Woman: I have cake and cookies. We also have some candy for later.
CD 1 Track 65
3. Man: Let me take you out and buy you a special dessert.
   Woman: That sounds great. What dessert?
   Man: I don't know. What do you want?
   Woman: How about an ice cream cone or a pie?
   Man: OK. We could also have a sundae if you want.

CD 1 Track 67, Page 60, Pronunciation
1. vegetables   **2.** sandwiches   **3.** nuts   **4.** potatoes

Unit 4
CD 2 Track 3, Page 63, Lesson 1, Exercise G
Maria has many things in her closet. You can see that she has three dresses. She also has a pair of shoes on the floor and one blouse next to the dresses. You can't see them, but Maria also has two coats in her closet. In the back, Maria has four pairs of pants.

CD 2 Track 6, Page 65, Lesson 2, Exercise D
Salesperson: We have many sizes and colors in our store. For example, in this shirt alone we have two extra-large blue shirts.
Yusuf: I don't need that size. Do you have any large white shirts?
Salesperson: Sure, we have one in the back. I can get it for you.
Yusuf: OK, and while you're at it, could you get me a medium green for my brother?
Salesperson: OK, but are you sure he might not want a small yellow shirt? We have three of those on sale.
Yusuf: I'm sure.

CD 2 Track 7, Page 67, Lesson 3, Exercise A

1. Cashier: Let's see. You want this comb and a candy bar. That's $1.00.
   Tien: $1.00?
   Cashier: That's right.
   Tien: OK. Here you go.

CD 2 Track 8

2. Cashier: OK, that's one red T-shirt.
   Tien: How much is it?
   Cashier: That's $6.25 with tax.

CD 2 Track 9

3. Cashier: Let's see. The shorts are $10.41.
   Tien: OK, do you have change?
   Cashier: Sure.
   Tien: Thanks!

CD 2 Track 11, Page 69, Lesson 3, Exercise E

1. Salesperson: Can I help you?
   Yusuf: Yes, I want this pair of pants.
   Salesperson: Great. Step this way.
   Yusuf: How much are they?
   Salesperson: They're $32.50.

CD 2 Track 12

2. Salesperson: Can I help you?
   Yusuf: Yes, I want a shirt. This one looks good.
   Salesperson: That's $24.50.

CD 2 Track 13

3. Salesperson: Can I help you?
   Maria: Yes, I need a pair of shoes for work.
   Salesperson: Here is a nice pair.
   Maria: How much are they?
   Salesperson: They are $44.00.

CD 2 Track 14

4. Salesperson: Can I help you?
   Maria: Yes I want a pair of shorts.
   Salesperson: Great. Step this way.
   Maria: How much are they?
   Salesperson: They are $18.00.

CD 2 Track 15

5. Salesperson: Can I help you?
   Maria: Yes, I need a dress for a party.
   Salesperson: What color are you looking for?
   Maria: Maybe black.
   Salesperson: How about this one?
   Maria: That's beautiful. How much is it?
   Salesperson: It's $82.50.

CD 2 Track 16

6. Salesperson: Can I help you?
   Maria: Yes, I'm looking for a blouse.
   Salesperson: What color are you looking for?
   Maria: Maybe yellow.
   Salesperson: How about this one?
   Maria: That's beautiful. How much is it?
   Salesperson: It's $22.50.

CD 2 Track 17, Page 70, Lesson 4, Exercise A

Here at Adel's Clothing Emporium we have great sales. Come in and see for yourself. Men's shirts in all sizes are only $22.50. You will be happy to see women's dresses in sizes 6 to 12 are only $40.00 a piece. We have men's sweaters on sale for $33.00. Men's pants are only $28.00 this week. Women's shoes are now only $24. Save $4! Blouses are a bargain at $18.00! We will be waiting for you. Remember Adel's Clothing Emporium for great savings!

CD 2 Track 19, Page 74, Lesson 5, Exercise D

Salesperson: Can I help you?
Ivan: Yes, I'm ready. I want to buy this dress for my wife.
Salesperson: That's $55.50.
Ivan: Do you take checks?
Salesperson: Of course!
Ivan: What's the date today?
Salesperson: June 4, 2005.
Ivan: Thanks.

CD 2 Track 21, Page 80 Pronunciation

1. pear   2. box   3. bay   4. pill

Unit 5

CD 2 Track 22, Page 81, Lesson 1, Exercise A

1. clothing store   2. shoe store   3. pharmacy
4. supermarket   5. video store

CD 2 Track 23, Page 81, Lesson 1, Exercise B

1. A: We need to go to the store.
   B: Why? What do we need?
   A: We need lots of things. We need milk, apples, and bread.
   B: Then we need to go to the supermarket right away.
   A: You said it!

CD 2 Track 24

2. A: My feet hurt.
   B. It's those shoes you're wearing.
   A: These things are old, but I love them.
   B: I think if we were to go to a shoe store, you would feel a lot better.
   A: OK, let's go.

CD 2 Track 25

3. A: I need a new dress for the party.
   B: What size do you wear?
   A: I wear a size 9.
   B: I think the clothing store on the corner has a big selection.
   A: Really? That's great. Let's go.

CD 2 Track 26

4. A: We need some medicine.
   B: Yes, I know. Could we go out and buy some aspirin?
   A: Sounds like a good idea. Let's get some bandages, too.
   B: OK, there's a pharmacy down the street.

CD 2 Track 27

5. A: There is a new movie on video. You've got to see it.
   B: Is it good?
   A: Yeah, it's great.
   B: OK, let's rent it. The video store is still open.

CD 2 Track 28, Page 82, Lesson 1, Exercise C

Excuse me, where's the hotel?
Where's a restaurant? I'm looking for the restaurant on Main Street.
Hi, there. Where's a fast-food place?
Excuse me, where's the clothing store?
I need new shoes. Where's the shoe store?
Hello. Where's the pharamacy?
Hi, where's the video store?
Do you know where the bus stop is?
Where's a telephone?

CD 2 Track 30, Page 86, Lesson 2, Exercise E

1. Hello, I'm Chen. I'm from China. I live in a house. I live on First Street in Alpine City.
2. Hi, I'm Latifa. I'm from Saudi Arabia. I live in an apartment in Casper Town on Parker Avenue.
3. It's nice to meet you. I'm Natalia. I'm from Guatemala. I live in a condominium in Alpine City on First Street.

CD 2 Track 32, Page 90, Lesson 4, Exercise A

1. I am James. I'm from the U.S. I live in a house. I take the bus to school.

CD 2 Track 33

2. I am Nga. I'm from Vietnam. I live in a house. I ride a bicycle to school.

CD 2 Track 34

3. I am Carina. I'm from Cuba. I live in an apartment. I drive to school.

CD 2 Track 37, Page 95, Lesson 5, Exercise J

1. Go straight. Turn right on Perry Avenue. It's next to Pete's Burgers.
2. Turn right on Hampton Street. Turn left on Second Street. It's next to Ned's Shoes.
3. Turn right on Hampton Street. It's next to El Marco Restaurant.
4. Go straight. Turn right on Perry Avenue. Turn right on Second Street. It's next Big's Foods.

CD 2 Track 39, Page 100, Pronunciation

1. bedroom   2. school   3. hospital   4. video

Unit 6

CD 2 Track 43, Page 103, Lesson 1, Exercise H

1. mouth   2. ear   3. neck   4. arm   5. head   6. foot

CD 2 Track 45, Page 104, Lesson 2, Exercise B

1. Doctor: It is so good to see you.
   Sang: It's good to see you, too.
   Doctor: What's the matter today?
   Sang: I have a terrible stomachache. Maybe I ate something bad yesterday.

CD 2 Track 46

2. Doctor: You look like you are in a lot of pain today.
   Mr. Jones: I sure am. Every day I get these terrible headaches. What can I do about it?
   Doctor: For headaches we usually prescribe pain relievers, but maybe we should check this out with some tests.
   Mr. Jones: Thanks, Doctor.

CD 2 Track 47

3. Doctor: How can I help you?
   Man: I think I have a high fever.
   Doctor: Let's check it out.
   Man: Thanks, Doctor. I hope I'm not too sick.

CD 2 Track 48

4. Doctor: You must be feeling terrible.
   Woman: I sure am. I have a runny nose. I think I only have a cold.
   Doctor: I know you want to go to work, but sometimes even with a cold, you need to take it easy for a few days.
   Woman: I guess you're right. I just hate staying home!

CD 2 Track 49

5. Doctor: Can I help you?
   Man: Yes, I can hardly move.
   Doctor: What seems to be the trouble?
   Man: I have a terrible backache.

CD 2 Track 50, Page 106, Lesson 2, Exercise F

1. Maritza is a good student. She can't come to school today because she has a headache. I hope she comes back tomorrow.

CD 2 Track 51

2. Shan works all day and comes to school at night. He isn't at school today. He called me and told me he would be out because he had a fever of 102 degrees. I hope he is all right and will get better soon.

CD 2 Track 52

3. Hi, John! This is your teacher Rob. I hear you're ill with a cold and a runny nose. It's no fun to be sick. Get well soon! Bye.

CD 2 Track 53

4. Anakiya can't go to work. She lifted some boxes yesterday, and now she has a backache. She's in bed and she can't get up.

CD 2 Track 54, Page 107, Lesson 3, Exercise B

Doctor: I'm a little late. I will be in the office in ten minutes. How many patients are there?
Receptionist: They are all waiting. Mrs. Hill and Mrs. Johnson are talking, and Antonio Espinosa is reading a magazine. Mr. Masters is sleeping.

Doctor: What are you doing?
Receptionist: I'm answering the phone and writing patient information in their files.
Doctor: OK, I'll see you in a few minutes.

CD 2 Track 55, Page 110, Lesson 4, Exercise A
Julio Rodriguez has an appointment at 3:30. He has a headache. His number is (777) 555-1395.
Huong Pham is coming in at 4:00. He has a high fever. His phone is 555-3311.
Richard Price has an appointment at 4:30. He has a stomachache. His number is 555-2323.
Mele Ikahihifo has a sore throat and a cough. She's coming in at 5:00.
Fred Wharton's number is 555-9764. He has a cold. He'll come at 5:30.
Ayumi Tanaka is coming in at 6:00 with a backache.

CD 2 Track 59, Page 120, Pronunciation
1. good   **2.** cold   **3.** lake   **4.** bag

Unit 7
CD 2 Track 63, Page 124 Lesson 2 Exercise B
1. Employee: Excuse me. Can I ask you a question?
  Manager: Sure.
  Employee: When do I take my lunch break?
  Manager: At 1 P.M.
  Employee: OK, thanks.
CD 2 Track 64
2. Nurse: Excuse me. Can you help me?
  Doctor: Sure.
  Nurse: What do I write on this line?
  Doctor: The patient's symptoms.
  Nurse: Thanks for your help.
CD 2 Track 65
3. Custodian: Excuse me. Can I ask you something?
  Co-worker: Sure.
  Custodian: Where do I find the mop to clean the floor?
  Co-worker: In the closet downstairs.
  Custodian: Thank you for your help.
CD 2 Track 66
4. Co-worker: Excuse me. Can you help me?
  Receptionist: Sure.
  Co-worker: Where do I put the mail when it comes in?
  Receptionist: In the boxes in the mail room.
  Co-worker: Thanks.

CD 2 Track 68, Page 126, Lesson 2, Exercise I
My name is Tan. I'm a custodian. I start work at 3:00 P.M. I work in a school.
CD 2 Track 69
My name is Maria. I'm a manager in a restaurant. I start work at 9:30 A.M.
CD 2 Track 70
My name is Alfredo. I'm a nurse. I work in a hospital. I start work at 6:00 P.M.

CD 2 Track 71, Page 127, Lesson 3, Exercise A
1. Receptionists have many responsibilities. They file and talk to customers. They also answer the phone.
CD 2 Track 72
2. A salesperson is important. He or she talks to customers and answers their questions.
CD 2 Track 73
3. Administrative assistants work in many different places. They do many different things. One of the important things they do is to type letters. Some administrative assistants can type more than 100 words a minute.
CD 2 Track 74
4. Custodians are very important. The custodian at the elementary school mops the floor three times a day. He empties the garbage and fixes broken chairs. He keeps the school clean.

CD 2 Track 75, Page 130, Lesson 4, Exercise B
1. Dear Mr. Chang, I'm sorry I can't come to work tomorrow. My child's sick. I can come to work on Wednesday. Sincerely, *Jim*
CD 2 Track 76
2. Dear Mr. Mitchell, I'm sorry I can't come to work tomorrow. I have a doctor's appointment. I can come to work on Wednesday. Sincerely, *Emilio Sanchez*
CD 2 Track 77
3. Dear Ms. Anderson, I'm sorry I can't come to school tomorrow. I have a family emergency. I can come to school on Wednesday. Sincerely, *Alexi*

CD 2 Track 78, Page 133, Lesson 5, Exercise A
Don't smoke. Don't eat. Wash your hands. Answer the phones. Type these letters. Don't file these papers.

CD 2 Track 80, Page 140, Pronunciation
1. We can't eat in class.   **2.** Tina can understand French.
3. I can meet you after work.   **4.** I can't type very well.

Unit 8
CD 2 Track 82, Page 142, Lesson 1, Exercise C
Liang: The teacher wants us to make special binders to study after school is finished.
Octavio: Yes, I know. We have to go to the store and buy some things. I don't think it is expensive.
Liang: We need binders first.
Octavio: What size do we need?
Liang: I think we need one-inch binders.
Octavio: Sounds good. They shouldn't be too big. (pause)
Liang: We need dividers, too.
Octavio: What are dividers?
Liang: You know, the heavy paper to make sections in your binder.
Octavio: Oh, yeah. How many do we need?
Liang: We need a set of five dividers. (pause)
Octavio: What else do we need?

Liang: We need paper for each section.
Octavio: How many sheets do we need?
Liang: Two hundred sheets, I think.
Octavio: That sounds right.

CD 2 Track 85, Page 147, Lesson 3, Exercise B
Paul: Excuse, where is Reams Office Supplies?
Linda: It's on First Street.
Paul: On First Street?
Linda: Yes, go straight on this street. Turn <u>right</u> on Main Street and <u>left</u> on First. It's <u>next to</u> the video store.
Paul: Thanks.

CD 2 Track 86, Page 150, Lesson 4, Exercise B
Carina: I have many goals. There are a lot of things that I want to accomplish. Right now, I'm focusing on daily goals. First, I need to exercise every day. I want to get up early and exercise one hour a day. It's important to be physically fit. I suppose that it's important to be prepared for school every day, too, so I'm going to study a lot. I plan to study for one hour every day even if I'm tired after work. I need to learn English and studying will help me do it faster. Somehow, I need to get plenty of sleep, too. Right now, I only sleep six hours a night, but my goal is to get eight hours of sleep. I hope I can do it. That's my goal. With all these goals, I will be healthy and I hope I will be successful at school.

CD 2 Track 87, Page 153, Lesson 5, Exercise A
Teachers and students share many duties or responsibilities. Among them are several very important things. For example, teachers and students should come to class on time. Students don't like to come early and find that the teacher is late. The teacher should come with a prepared lesson every day. That's also very important. Students have more confidence in a teacher who is prepared. The teacher helps the students, but students can also teach each other. Students should study at home. There is a lot that they can study. For example, they can study new words at home. Sometimes the teacher gives homework. Students who do their homework learn English faster.

CD 2 Track 89, Page 160, Pronunciation
1. choose   2. wash   3. ships   4. catch

Stand Out Basic Skills Index

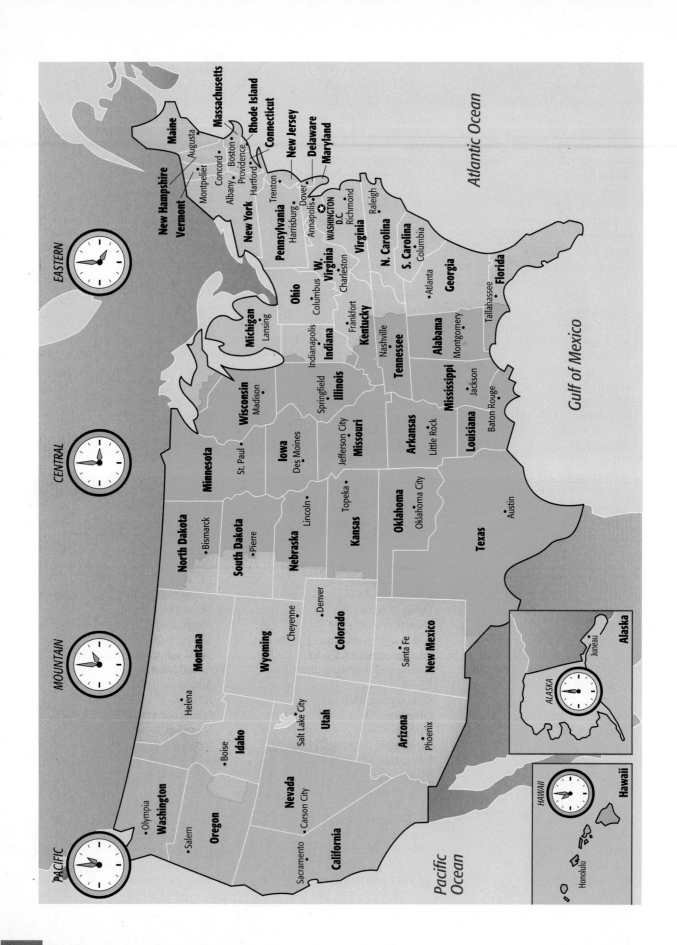